# The Modern Practice
# of Adult Education

SUNY Series, Teacher Empowerment and School Reform
Henry A. Giroux and Peter L. McLaren, editors

# The Modern Practice of Adult Education

*A Postmodern Critique*

Derek Briton

STATE UNIVERSITY OF NEW YORK PRESS

Published by
State University of New York Press, Albany

©1996  State University of New York

For information, address State University of New York Press,
State University Plaza, Albany, NY 12246

Production by Christine Lynch
Marketing by Dana E. Yanulavich

**Library of Congress Cataloging-in-Publication Data**

Briton, Derek, 1953–
    The modern practice of adult education: a postmodern critique /
Derek Briton.
        p.   cm. — (SUNY series, teacher empowerment and school
reform)
    Includes bibliographical references and index.
    ISBN 0–7914–3026–X (pb : alk. paper). — ISBN 0–7914–3025–1 (ch :
alk. paper)
    1. Adult education—Philosophy.  2. Critical pedagogy.
3. Postmodernism.  4. Adult education—Research.  I. Title.
II. Series: Teacher empowerment and school reform.
LC5219.B723  1996
374'.001—dc20                                                    95-38597
                                                                          CIP

10 9 8 7 6 5 4 3 2 1

At a time when the furthermost corner of the globe has been conquered by technology and opened to economic exploitation; when any incident whatever, regardless of where or when it occurs, can be communicated to the rest of the world at any desired speed; when the assassination of a king in France and a symphony concert in Tokyo can be "experienced" simultaneously; when time has ceased to be anything other than velocity, instantaneousness, and simultaneity, and time as history has vanished from the lives of all peoples'; when a boxer is regarded as a nation's great man; when mass meetings attended by millions are looked on as a triumph—then, yes then, through all this turmoil a question still haunts us like a specter: What for?—Whither?—And what then?

—Heidegger, 1959, pp. 37–38

# Contents

# *Preface*

It should be merely a commonplace,
recognized by everyone, that in the
case of a work of reflection, removing
the scaffolding and cleaning up the
area around the building not only is of
no benefit to the reader, but deprives
[her or] him of something essential.
Unlike the work of art, there is no finished edifice here, nor an edifice to be
finished; just as much as, and even
more than the results, what is important is the work of reflection and it is
perhaps mostly this that an author can
make us see, if he can make us see anything at all.

—Castoriadis, 1987, p. 9

A disjuncture between the modern instrumental practice of adult education and my own understanding of this field of endeavor, an understanding based on my personal experiences as an adult learner, provided the inspiration for this text. The result is a work that calls into
question the moral integrity of the modern practice of adult education
and the modernist perspective that informs it. In terms of content, the
text first identifies a number of adult educators who have voiced their
discontent with the field's dominant vision; argues for adult educators
to look beyond the narrow, technicist concepts that guide contemporary

thinking and action; describes a number of difficulties associated with relinquishing the model of understanding that informs this instrumental perspective; and proposes an alternative model of understanding to inform the practice of adult education. It then discusses the moral and political implications of adult education; examines the relationships among knowledge, values, and science; exposes science's ideological roots; offers a historical critique of scientism; and argues that since a disinterested, scientific vision of adult education cannot be sustained legitimately, it should be reconceptualized as the cultural practice it has always been. It next traces the origins of the model of understanding that underlies modern science's instrumental perspective to the appearance of the modern subject, offering extracts from Marx, Nietzsche, Elias, and Heidegger to reveal the sociohistorical underpinnings of this distinctively modern sense of self. Following upon this, it identifies four theoretical paradigms that can be employed to inform practice and research—positivist, interpretive, critical, and postmodern—and addresses the problems associated with establishing the respective value of each of these perspectives. It concludes with an appeal to adult educators to reconceptualize their endeavor as a postmodern pedagogy of engagement; offers an example of such a pedagogy; discusses the implications of this vision for practice; and culminates in a brief postscript, wherein the author reflects on his interrogation of the disjuncture that inspired the text.

It would be a mistake, however, to judge the text's worth solely in terms of its content. The central intent of the work is to introduce adult educators to what Cornelius Castoriadis (1987, pp. 2–3), in the citation that introduces this section, refers to as "the work of reflection." Yet this aim was far from clear when the work was first undertaken. To those of a modernist persuasion, such an admission may be more than a little disconcerting. Does not the author, after all, need to be clear about what it is that he or she hopes to achieve and about just how he or she hopes to achieve that end *before* the work is begun? In keeping with such reasoning, the typical modernist work either presents its product in the guise of a perfect hermetic structure or promotes its mode of construction as a rigorous logical process—adult education texts have proven exemplary in conforming to this standard. But as I was soon to learn, and Castoriadis (pp. 2–3) makes clear, such totalizing strategies serve only to ensnare rather than release the thinker from modernity's epistemic grip, persuading the author to participate in and promulgate the "disastrous illusion towards which he [or she], like all of us, is already naturally inclined": that readers need only, if they so desire, move in and occupy the theoretical edifice the author has constructed before them as if it were their very own. Why does this present such a problem? Because it peremptorily renders critical inquiry and careful reflection obsolete. Thinking, Castoriadis tells us, entails much more than "building cathedrals or composing symphonies," contending that "if the symphony exists, it is the reader who must create it in his own ears."

Viewed in this light, the predicament of adult educators who find themselves at odds with the modern instrumental practice of adult education takes on a different hue. If the critiques such educators generate simply conform to the modernist form, that is, present themselves as seamless totalities or portray themselves in terms of an unerring logic, they will unwittingly serve to reproduce that which they wish to renounce. If they wish to avoid this performative contradiction, those who dare to question modern adult education's instrumental practices must develop a different way of thinking, a way of calling into question not only the concrete practices of modern adult education but also the modernist structures of thinking that shape and legitimate those practices. This demands a new textual form, since such a way of thinking cannot be simply bequeathed to others as a fait accompli—"If the symphony exists, it is the reader who must create it in his own ears."

This text comprises an attempt to develop such a textual form, a form that does not seek to deny its conjectural foundations, to mask its tenuous structure, to protect its precarious integrity. It begins with an account of the struggle that ensued when I, an adult educator far from enamoured with the modern instrumental practice of adult education, first wrestled with the problem of developing a critique of such practices from *within* the prevailing modernist structure of thinking. This struggle, which would be dismissed normally as a prelude to the work proper, constitutes what Castoriadis (1987) calls the "scaffolding" and "rubble" of the "work of reflection." While it could, and undoubtedly would, be excised from a typical modernist text as something superfluous to the finished product, omitting the scaffolding and debris that attest to this struggle would unquestionably deprive the reader of something essential. For it is during this struggle that the text's intent and structure is transformed and it assumes the form of a work of reflection.

It was the realization that any critique of the modern practice of adult education and the modernist perspective that informs it that purports to be "definitive" is necessarily culpable—that is, guilty of a performative contradiction because it claims to be that which it emphatically denies: beyond question and above reproach—that precipitated the restructuring of the text's intent and form. Rather than simply provide insurmountable "proof" of its failings, the text engages the reader in recurring critiques of the modern practice of adult education. This provides the reader not with incontestable "evidence" that *must* be ingested whole, but a range of opportunities to come to grips, through the work of reflection, with the many unquestioned assumptions, inconsistencies, and contradictions that inform the modern practice of adult education. Such an approach has the additional benefit of accommodating the protests that inevitably surface whenever beliefs, no matter how erroneous, are initially challenged, no matter how incontrovertible the proof. This irrational privileging of belief over knowledge—of disavowal—is something critical works must address if they do not wish to be simply rejected out of hand.[1] Recognizing that even seemingly incontestable empirical proofs carry little weight in the face of disavowal, the text presents arguments for their *heuristic* rather than factual worth. While, for example, the *factual* worth of an argument always remains in question—given the practice of disavowal and the probabilistic nature of empirical evidence—its heuristic worth is readily calculable: a direct reflection of how well it exposes the inadequacies of the position it interrogates by unveiling the assumptions, inconsistencies, and contradictions at play.

It is in seeking to include and engage the reader in the work of reflection that the text assumes a form that distinguishes it markedly from its modernist counterparts. In favoring commentary over empirical evidence, a multiplicity of voices over a prescriptive narrative, the development of an ethical attitude *toward* practice over formulaic prescriptions *for* practice, and inter- over intra-disciplinary literature to support its claims, the work calls into question a whole range of modernist predilections. In so doing, the text inverts the modernist urge to privilege the nomothetic and absolute over the idiographic and conjectural and demonstrates how the tenets of modern adult education practice can be called into question from an ethical, *post*modern perspective that appeals to alternative, but equally valid, forms of evidence.

While the text repeatedly calls the modern practice of adult education into question, its intent and structure make it clear to the reader that the task of critical adult educators is *not* simply to resurrect some long repressed and silenced body of "authentic" practices that lies dormant somewhere beneath and beyond the "inauthentic" practices that dominate the field today. Rather, adult education practices are represented as intertwined, juxtaposed, and at odds with one another—practices that can and often do proceed unaware of and to the exclusion of one another. In emphasizing the *discontinuous* nature of adult education practices and repeatedly breaching the narrowly prescribed parameters of adult education's orthodoxy, the text confirms its *post*modern stance. In so doing, it opens the modern practice of adult education to a range of important debates that are of significant import to adult educators. In keeping with its postmodern thrust, the text resists synthesizing these disparate discourses into a master narrative that elides their differences and unites their purpose. The text's multiplicity of voices also serves to identify progressive voices from within the field of adult education, relate these voices to their critical counterparts from outside the field, and provide a well-documented record of critical texts that adult educators can draw upon to help them develop their own work of reflection.

The text's central arguments could, undoubtedly, be otherwise structured, presented, and substantiated; the intent of the work, after all, is not to offer a definitive account of how adult education *should* proceed but to promote serious thinking and debate within the field about the implications and consequences of unquestioningly embracing the modern instrumental practice of adult education. In recapitulating my own struggle with "the work of reflection," I hope to encourage other adult educators to engage in their own. By repeatedly demonstrating how seemingly necessary truths, when closely examined and tested, collapse in upon themselves to reveal another "truth," which, in turn, can be interrogated to the point that it, too, inverts and yields yet another path to explore, and so on ad infinitum, the text reveals its object of analysis to be not just the modern practice of adult education but the very experience of interpretation—the work of reflection. This displaces the worth of the text, its value, from its message to its mode of analysis and the interrogations that mode of analysis fosters and promotes. In demonstrating the fleeting and transitory nature of the Real, the text hopes to alert the reader to the fact that it is in the light of what they *do*, not what they once did or profess to do, that the ideas of adult educators and the institution of adult education must be judged. The Real, ever fluid and vital, continually evades our attempts to place strictures around it, despite our insatiable desire to do so. In linguistic terms, educators must be willing to interrogate their ideas as active verbs rather than passive nouns if they wish to avoid denuding human experience of its creative potential:

> The educator, artist or even doctor does not "know" the final result he/she seeks; nor does he/she simply follow material lines of force, as if they could be somehow read directly from the given, as if the given were immediately and univocally signifying, as in the dream world of the positivist. There is an indeterminateness in every praxis: the project is changed as it encounters the materiality of the world; and the visage of the world is altered once my project contacts it. (Howard, 1977, p. 287)

# Acknowledgments

It would be impossible to acknowledge all the people who have made contributions to this work. There is a nucleus of people, however, who deserve special mention. Without their assistance this work would never have materialized. To Gail, my partner and wife, I am especially indebted. Without her endless patience, boundless understanding, and unflinching support, this project would have remained forever an idea. To Dean, Alex, and Clare, my children, I am especially grateful for their patience and understanding. My special thanks to Don Plumb, my dearest friend and associate, who listened to me more than anyone should have to and encouraged me more than anyone could be expected to. Thanks also to Marlene Lewis and Lee J. Lewis-Plumb, who conspired with my family to keep me sane by making me take time to play, even when I didn't want to.

# 1

# Engaging the Question
# of Adult Education

No good can come from avoiding the
essential issue. There is a deep-seated
conflict in this country concerning
adult education and we may as well
confront it. . . . There exists at present
two schools of thought with respect to
adult education. . . . The first, I shall
call "mechanistic" and the second the
"organic." . . . Those who represent the
*mechanistic* viewpoint seem to believe
that adult education . . . always means
extending something which is already
here. . . . The ideas with which they
surround adult education are consequently quantitative, if not static in
character. At best, such persons seem
to think of adult education in naively
instrumental terms. . . . On the other
hand, those who hold the *organic* point
of view assume at the outset that adult
education . . . is not merely "more of
the same"; that is, an extension of
something which the privileged
already enjoy, but rather a new quality
and a new dimension in education . . . ,
a right, a normal expectancy, and not
charity. Its purpose is to do something
for adults which cannot be achieved by
conventional education.
                    —Lindeman, 1938b, p. 49

1

That the field of adult education is a contested terrain, a site of political struggle, was clear to Eduard Lindeman over half a century ago. That it remains so today is no longer readily apparent: an instrumental or "mechanistic" vision of adult education has come to dominate the field. I learned this quickly when I began my studies in adult and higher education. This instrumental understanding of adult education, however, contrasted starkly with the understanding that I brought to the field, an understanding tempered by my own experience as an adult learner. Unable to accommodate my direct experience within the field's vocation-centered, instrumental vision, I subsequently found myself driven to question its integrity.

Because I had returned to school after a number of years in the workforce as a tradesperson and union leader, not to amass more technical knowledge, further my administrative skills, or increase my earning power, but to pursue a general arts degree, I knew that not *all* adults construe education as an essentially vocational endeavor to be pursued in purely instrumental terms. As an adult learner, I had looked to education to broaden my understanding, not to better equip me for the marketplace. When, as an undergraduate, I switched first from psychology to English, and then from English to philosophy, I had done so *not* to increase my chances of employment, but to accommodate my changing interests. While my motives for changing programs seemed perfectly rational to me, when I tried to defend them to former workmates or fellow students, I quickly learned that, for many of them, rationality correlated directly with employability, not interest. I was one of a shrinking few, it seemed, who considered education an end in itself, rather than a means to an end—employment. While the issue of employability had always been a matter of concern to me, contributing, for instance, to my decision to investigate and pursue graduate studies in adult and higher education, it had never been my prime concern.

In fact, after completing an honors degree in philosophy, I had decided to pursue a master's degree in the same discipline, reasoning that if all went well, there was a good chance that I might enter a doctoral program in the future. After one semester, however, my situation changed, and the possibility of studying beyond the master's level began to look remote. My situation was such that I had to suspend my studies, and this allowed me, among other things, time to investigate my options. At this point, I have to admit that I stumbled on adult education quite inadvertently—a career in the education of adults being something that simply had not occurred to me. I was immediately intrigued by the prospect, however, recalling that I had presented a number of workshops and training programs to adults as a union leader and that I had instructed a number of adult apprentices as a journeyperson. Moreover, as president of my local union, I had served as a trustee and chairperson of an education training fund for a number of years. I excitedly discussed this new option with Gail, my wife—without whose support, both emotional and financial, my sojourn into academia would have been impossible—and subsequently made the decision to apply for admission into the graduate program in adult and higher education.

After my application for admission proved successful, I entered my new field of study eager to supplement my rudimentary knowledge of adult education. But the modern practice of adult education, I quickly learned, did not reflect my own lived experience as an adult learner; moreover, it took for granted much that I, as a student of the humanities, had learned to question. I began, therefore, investigating alternative visions of adult education, only to learn that a number of adult educators shared my concerns and were involved in an ongoing struggle to reconceptualize the field's "mechanistic" vision of adult education. I also learned that an "organic" vision of adult education had once rivalled the instrumental perspective that dominates the field today, and that Eduard Lindeman, over fifty years ago, had articulated a vision of adult education that not only accommodated my experience as an adult learner but also echoed many of my concerns regarding the modern practice of adult education. Lindeman, I learned, had staunchly opposed those who sought to reduce adult education to a range of "mechanistic" practices, absolutely refusing to view it as a vocational enterprise to be pursued in purely instrumental terms. Lindeman's was a vision of adult education that resonated with my own.

For Lindeman (1935b), adult education is "a social process . . . , not . . . a simple device whereby knowledge is transferred from one mind to another" (p. 45). Its "primary goal is not vocational. Its aim is not to teach people how to make a living but rather how to live. It offers no ulterior reward. . . . Life is its fundamental subject matter" (1929, p. 37). Adult education, he argues, is "social education for purposes of social change . . . , an instrument designed to shorten the 'cultural lag' . . . in a democratic society" (1945a, pp. 116–117), "a mode of social adaption . . . ; the answer to blind prejudice and demagoguery" (1944c, p. 102). It is "not merely . . . a means for increasing the efficiency or the smartness of a few selected individuals," but rather "an instrument for social change" (1938b, p. 51), "a cultural adventure aiming at freedom through intelligence" (1949, p. 179), an endeavor that "begins where vocational education leaves off. Its purpose is to put meaning into the whole of life" (1961, p. 5). Against those who promote it as simply "a matter of adapting individuals to existing cultural norms," Lindeman argues that adult education, "on the contrary, . . . is definitely futuristic, in movement towards coming adjustments" (1944c, p. 94). It is an indispensable way "of shortening our cultural lag," of bridging "the distance between our technological advances and our cultural values" (1944d, p. 111), of ensuring the continuation of freedom and democracy in our modern age.

An avid student of history, Lindeman (1937, pp. 75–76) knew from ages past that "when the distance between life as action and life as reflection becomes so great that experience loses its organic wholeness societies begin to disintegrate." He also knew that "unhappily, we live in such an age," recognizing that "we . . . have lost the essential connection between our vast technological equipment and the sense of human value. Our civilization has outrun our culture; our means have become inconsistent with our ends." In such times, Lindeman contends—times characterized by a growing "discrepancy between the two major departments of experience, namely the outer, external, objective aspects of life, and the inner, psychological, subjective processes by means of which experience is evaluated"—democratic societies are faced with a major challenge: "to discover sanctions for peace and order other than violence." This challenge, Lindeman argues, can only be met through adult education. There is "no other alternative," he contends: "the equation ends with experimental social education," with adult education that "consists of *increased awareness of the self and of other selves, directed toward social justice.*"

Convinced that "social justice cannot be achieved through the learning of children and youth," since "the young make their adaptions to an adult-controlled world," Lindeman (1937, pp. 76–77) maintains that adult education is the only "instrument of action" that can establish a just social order. Adults, he contends, *must* "change while education for the young is being improved"; otherwise, "we become entangled in a vicious circle." Adult education, therefore, "is not only merely education of adults; adult education is learning associated with social purposes"—its "complete objective is to synchronize the democratic and the learning processes"; it is "the operating alternative for dominance, dictatorship, and violence." In adult education, "the adult learner," Lindeman argues, "is not merely engaged in the pursuit of knowledge" but is "experimenting with himself," is "testing his incentives in the light of knowledge," is, "in short, changing his habits, learning to live on behalf of new motivations." While today, Lindeman's exclusionary pronouns cry out to be replaced with more inclusionary terms, this should not distract us from the importance of his message: adult education is a distinctively social endeavor.

Lindeman, in fact, dismisses "mechanistic" adult education as ingenuous for this very reason, cautioning his fellow Americans that "if it turns out to be impossible to induce considerable numbers of American adults to subject themselves to a learning procedure which is social in its aims as well as its methods, our society will be remade by force and violence." Against those who argue that "in an age of increasing tensions . . . the function of education is to ease and relieve those tensions," Lindeman (1944d, pp. 105–106) contends that "it is the function of education to understand the ideas and the needs which have precipitated the tensions," that "each tension is . . . an educational opportunity," and that "to evade social tensions is to invite trouble." Conceptions of adult education that fail to recognize its irremediably social nature, Lindeman (1944d, p. 101) argues, are intrinsically flawed, convinced that "the purpose of adult education is to prevent intellectual statics; the arrested development of individuals who have been partially educated cannot be prevented otherwise." Proponents of "mechanistic" adult education, of educational practices that encourage individuals to act "on behalf of goals and purposes with which they have had nothing to do," Lindeman (1938a, p. 147) warns, are courting disaster. Adult education, like democracy, Lindeman (1938a, p. 151) maintains, "is neither a goal nor a mechanical device for attaining a preconceived goal. It is at bottom a mode of life founded upon the assumption that goals and methods, means and ends, must be compatible and complementary." To separate means from ends, facts from values, Lindeman (1944a, p. 160) warns, is to forget that "the ends . . . 'pre-exist in the means'," that "we become what we do, not what we wish." To "violate this principle," to succumb to "the doctrine that the end justifies the means," is to abandon our "democratic faith" and be left standing "on dubious moral ground."

In the preface to *Learning Democracy*, Stephen Brookfield (1987) notes of Lindeman that "throughout his life he argued against the dangers of over-specialization of functions and interests, which he saw as perhaps the single most distressing consequence of the technological changes of the twentieth century." He was convinced that "specialization produced truncated, inchoate individuals, whose lives were characterized by a schizophrenic split between personal concerns and broader social movements." While recognizing that "we are committed . . . to the process of division of labor, to specialism," Lindeman (1961, pp. 81–84) rails against "experts and specialists whose functions become external to the people whom they serve," identifying them as "miseducated . . . 'particularists' . . . who behave as if 'one phase of the process' were 'the source of all others'." Their "educative contact," he contends, "is forever education in a false direction," for "the specialist who becomes protagonist for a particularist point of view has already deserted the spirit of science" and "labors under the 'illusion of centrality' which keeps him and his disciples from recognizing 'that the life process is an evolving whole of mutually interacting parts, any of which is effect as well as cause'." While cognizant of the tantalizing allure of instrumental education to those enamored with the twin goals of technological and economic "progress," Lindeman (1961, p. 49) relentlessly challenges their construal of adult education as simply another means of producing the army of specialists that "progress" demands. Fearing that they "may . . . so far exaggerate the incentives and motives which are derived from capitalism and profit production as to cause the entire educational system to become a direct response to this system and to lead to its further emphasis," Lindeman warns that if this emergent "system, both on its economic and educational sides, becomes too rigid and too oppressive and incapable of sincere self-criticism, nothing short of violent revolution will suffice to change its direction." For this very reason, Lindeman rejects as inherently dangerous the view that adult educators need only be technicians skilled in the science of learning.

Lindeman, Brookfield (1987, pp. 12–13) notes, recommends that adult educators be schooled not only in motivational and developmental psychology but also in "cultural history, since motives for learning are affected by the intellectual climate of an era, which is itself related intimately to contemporary social movements." They should "be capable of understanding the work experience of their students" and "be equipped to interpret and build on the inter- and intra-relationship of various disciplines of knowledge"; they should not be specialists in one area of knowledge: "a liberal grasp of a wide range of subject areas and interpretive frameworks was necessary to a good teacher of adults." Adult education, Lindeman (1929b, p. 23) argues, "is not a process of acquiring the tools of learning . . . , but rather a way of learning the relation between knowledge and living. Adult education is functional in the sense that its aim is to serve individual and group adjustment, but it is non-vocational." It "begins not with subject-matter but with the situations and experiences which mold adult life." It is "a method whereby the experiences and ideologies of adults are freed from traditional bonds." Consequently,

> during the years when Thorndike, Lorge and others were assessing the physiological and psychological bases for *excellent* adult learning, Lindeman was describing the special character and the depth of mature learning. He did not look upon learning merely as some kind of social *governor* or control: primarily it was itself dynamic; essentially it meant change and growth. (Kidd, 1961, p. xvii)

Unswerving in his insistence that it not be (mis)construed as a purely instrumental practice that serves simply to bolster and legitimate the existing social order, Lindeman maintains that adult education can be understood properly only as

> a co-operative venture in non-authoritarian, informal learning the chief purpose of which is to discover the meaning of experience; a quest of the mind which digs down to the roots of the preconceptions which formulate our conduct; a technique of learning for adults which makes education coterminous with life, and hence elevates living itself to the level of an experiment. (Lindeman, 1925, cited in Stewart, 1984, p. 1)

Consequently, "to Lindeman the current interest in adult education using distance teaching methods and educational broadcasting," not to mention "individual computer usage, would have been not only inexplicable but also a contradiction in terms" (Brookfield, 1987, p. 5). Lindeman, Brookfield suggests, would have scorned such activities "as mass instruction or programmed instruction," as practices devoid of "the collaborative articulation and interpretation of experience claimed by him as the quintessential adult educational activity." Despite all claims to the contrary, then, Lindeman (1945a, p. 117) refuses to believe that adult educators can abrogate their moral responsibility and pursue their enterprise in a purely instrumental manner, convinced that she or "he who deals with the needs of life plunges into that icy pool which so many would like to avoid, the name of which is morality."

It was, then, somewhat of a relief, after spending several months learning that university courses in adult and higher education were courses concerned almost exclusively with questions of technique, to find in Lindeman confirmation of my own experience and concerns as an adult learner. For, by that time, I had learned that my unease with the dominant vision of adult education was something neither faculty nor my fellow students shared. Expediency, I had learned, was the order of the day: to spend time debating whether a certain course of action *should* be pursued or not was considered a waste of time. After all, institutions or employers made those sorts of "messy" political decisions. Adult educators need only concern themselves with *how* adults learn, not *why*. The modern practice of adult education, I had been assured, is a scientific enterprise, an endeavor untainted by moral and political imperatives. Value judgments, questions of intrinsic worth, notions of the common good are metaphysical (my word, not theirs) issues, I had been told, theoretical concerns that are of little consequence to a field of study committed to the "practical" dimension of life.[1]

But while I gained some solace in reading Lindeman, I also came to realize that to replace adult education's obsessive preoccupation with *how* adults learn with a genuine concern for *what* they should learn would require more than a rebuttal of its scientific underpinnings. For while the conflict Lindeman identified in adult education fifty-five years ago remains unresolved to this day, there is a major difference between the modern practice of adult education and the nascent field of practice Lindeman described: the "mechanistic" school of thought has come to dominate the field to such an extent that all "organic" visions of adult education have been relegated to the margins. The instrumental perspective that now informs the modern practice of adult education has become so entrenched in modern consciousness that its reified concepts now appear sacrosanct. The commonsense assumption that the modern practice of adult education is a disinterested, *scientific* endeavor that need not, indeed, *should not* concern itself with moral and political questions has become all but impossible to question because the field's normative base can no longer be addressed within its narrowly defined, depoliticized, dehistoricized, technicist, professional discourse.

With these factors in mind, I realized that any convincing critique of the modern practice of adult education would have to do more than undermine the world view that informs the field's technicist, professionalized discourse; it would have to identify the factors, the forces, and the conditions that prompt adult educators and adult learners to accept an instrumental vision of adult education, even though to do so is to abandon the ideals of democracy and submit to a growing loss of personal freedom. In an address to a gathering of adult educators, Lindeman (1938b, p. 49) suggested that the increasing acceptance of "mechanistic" adult education may be attributable to a failure, on the part of adult educators, to clearly articulate the "organic" nature and social purpose of their endeavor:

> it seems inescapably clear that people do not know what we mean by adult education. Their confusion does not derive from lack of awareness that adults are capable of study; what they do not fully and clearly comprehend is why adults *should* study. As adult educators we have not been clear in our own minds, and consequently the situation with respect to motivation for adult learning is one of muddled confusion.

Yet while Lindeman is willing to entertain the idea that "perhaps we have all along been using the wrong word," recognizing that "adult education is a prosaic term which seems to place emphasis upon genetics rather than upon educational aims," he notes that, ultimately, "the word itself cannot possibly be our main difficulty because language, being always responsive to changing meanings, is flexible and we can make the term mean whatever we choose." He concludes, therefore, that "the real difficulty lies deeper than the mere use of words." Brookfield (1987) offers an indication of just how much deeper this difficulty lies.

A number of commentators, Brookfield (1987, p. 196) notes, have attempted to draw attention to the "lack of discourse among adult educators of the important social and political issues of the day." He notes, however, that "part of the reason for this silence was the manner by which adult educators adopted an adaptive rationale—'to let arrangements replace goals . . .'—in their programming activities." Adult educators, Brookfield contends, "under the pressure of producing a self-financing program . . . , fell foul all too often to the temptation of allowing the criteria of increased enrollments and revenues to determine the direction of their efforts." The "deeper difficulty," then, seems to be that adult educators, isolated within the confines of the field's depoliticized, decontextualized, instrumental discourse, have lost sight of the political and economic factors that are determining the fate of their enterprise. Any convincing critique of the modern practice of adult education, it seemed to me, then, would have to address not only this "deeper difficulty" but also *why* some adult educators feel justified, and others even compelled, to relinquish their moral responsibility. Simply to demonstrate that instrumental adult education is not a purely disinterested scientific endeavor but rather a value-laden, political practice that serves to perpetuate the status quo, would do little to change the minds of those who embrace the modern practice of adult education. A much more persuasive critique would be one that revealed the intrinsically social nature and moral underpinnings of the technicist world view, a critique that identified not only how the forces and conditions that now serve to mystify those underpinnings came into being but also why they continue to exist.

My hope is that the research undertaken herein will contribute to the development of just such a persuasive critique of the modern practice of adult education. However, it remains highly unlikely that critique, alone, no matter how persuasive or how well substantiated, will ever be sufficient to displace the field's deeply entrenched technicist ideas, ideas that arose from, and continue to be supported by, very real material conditions. While critical reflection may provide an incentive to question prevailing practices, there is much to suggest that the ideas that inform those practices, once reified, can be overturned only when the social forms that support them are changed. This means that alternative adult education practices—democratic and emancipatory forms of adult education that embody the ideals they promote, for instance— must emerge to engender and support the ideas that inform them *before* any real possibility of displacing the field's reified, technicist ideas will present itself. The critique presented, herein, is more a justification to pursue alternative adult education practices, then, than an argument to change minds. There are, of course, very real problems associated with putting democratic and emancipatory ideals into practice in the classroom, but these problems must be addressed if any real changes are to occur.

# 2

# *The Fear of Falling into Error*

> If the fear of falling into error intro-
> duces an element of distrust into sci-
> ence [systematic inquiry], which with-
> out any scruples of that sort goes on
> and actually does know, it is not easy
> to understand why, conversely, a dis-
> trust should not be placed in this very
> distrust, and why we should not take
> care lest the fear of error is not just the
> initial error. *As a matter of fact, this*
> *fear presupposes something, indeed a*
> *great deal, as truth, and supports its*
> *scruples and consequences on what*
> *should itself be examined beforehand*
> *to see whether it is truth.*
> —Hegel, 1807, in Hegel, 1974, p. 45,
> emphasis added

## TECHNICISM AND ITS DISCONTENTS

The central ideas expressed in this text are ideas that I believed were important before I became an adult educator, and they are ideas that I continue to believe are important as an adult educator. They are what many refer to as fundamental ideas, ideas that concern themselves with the nature of human beings, freedom, truth, power, the role of science and technology in the modern world, and how human beings come to know themselves, one another, and their world. These are ideas that have framed and continue to frame my thinking, and they are ideas this

13

work gives me the opportunity to pursue.[1] My conviction that adult educators should give serious consideration to these fundamental ideas was most recently reinforced by events I witnessed in Saskatoon, in July of 1991.

While attending the 23rd Annual International Conference of the Community Development Society, I was struck by the fact that many of the social, healthcare, and community workers in attendance were highly critical of the manner in which

> our technologically advanced societies have placed an almost blind faith in what is euphemistically called "the law of the instrument"; namely, the belief that the only route to problem solving lies in ever-larger outlays of capital in technology and in an endless upgrading of technical, professional and managerial skills. (Campfens, 1991, pp. 7–8)

A number of conferees, calling upon poignant examples from their own past, confirmed what many others had come to suspect: that "techno-logical progress, once hailed by millions as the panacea for virtually all of humanity's problems—and not merely its material problems—not only failed to solve a number of material and nonmaterial problems but became a principal problem in itself" (Ohliger, 1990, pp. 629–630). As a result, many of those in attendance voiced suspicions and concerns about

> the primacy we have placed on modern science and technology and the extent to which we have come to rely on the rationality and exper-tise of the trained professional and technocrat in addressing human need and solving problems, to the near exclusion of the potential that lies within mutual aid and social mobilization. (Campfens, 1991, p. 7)

As I listened to the concerns conference participants expressed about the technicization and professionalization of community devel-opment, I recognized a parallel between their concerns and my own regarding the modern practice of adult education. Such concerns have been expressed by a growing number of adult educators in the last ten years. Welton (1987b), for instance, laments the fact that "Canadian adult education, with notable exceptions, is professionalized, becalmed, and technicized" (p. 29). As opposed to "the educational radicals of the 1930s and 1940s," educators who "rejected liberal, individualistic educational ideals," educators who took "a stand on the fundamental issues of the day," today's adult educators, Welton contends, educators who "are captive to ideologies of the individual learner," educators who "lack a coherent understanding of the social purpose of adult education," educators who "are fragmented along institutional lines," are educators who see themselves "as professionals marketing programs and not as activists mobilizing people through dialogue" (pp. 29–30). In order to halt this psychologization, depoliticization, and bureaucratization of the field, adult educators, Welton (1991, p. 25) argues, "must reject the idea that 'adult education' has an essence that only need be represented in appropriate, value-neutral scientific language." He rejects unreservedly the very possibility of disinterested knowledge, pointing out that the concept of "adult education" is formed, is "made visible, given a body, only when it is constituted by a 'discursive field' (ideas, texts, theories, use of language)." Convinced "that 'adult education' as a professional practice was constructed quite consciously to exclude socialism (viewed as dangerous knowledge)," Welton warns us that "particular discursive practices are intimately bound up with social power and control"; he continues:

> knowledge/power, Foucault has taught us, cannot be thought apart. This insight demands that we pay attention to the way adult education discourse sets the limits on what counts as authentic educational practice, and perhaps more important, social and political action. Adult educational discourses might be read as a very important way that our society organises its power relations. (1991, p. 26)

Sharing many of Welton's (1991, 1987b) concerns, Collins (1991, pp. 2–4) is another adult educator who argues against the modern technicist conception of adult education: "the cult of efficiency" that "is most pronounced in North American adult education practice." According to Collins:

> the cult of efficiency refers to a growing, and seductive, tendency to make more and more areas of human endeavour (the practical, moral, and political projects of everyday life) amenable to measurement and techno-bureaucratic control according to what is invoked as a scientific approach. It elevates technical rationality to a position of undisputed pre-eminence over other forms of human thought and discourse.

Deeply suspicious of this modern "proclivity to incorporate within the field of practice an increasing array of pedagogical techniques," Collins argues against *technicism*: "the growing tendency towards inappropriate applications of technical, mechanistic formats . . . to steer adult education endeavours." In a later work, Collins (1992, p. 18) concludes that "a sense of solidarity, rather than a misplaced yearning for professionalized status, is necessary to sustain continuing resistance against the ideology of technique enshrined within modern adult education." With this in mind, he suggests that "it would be helpful to restore the vision of adult education as 'friends educating each other' along with the kind of pedagogy expressed in the work of Paulo Freire and Thomas Hodgskin.[2] Such a pedagogy," he maintains, "is ethically concerned, anti-technicist, and clearly counter-hegemonic . . . , a matter for political commitment as well as philosophical insight."

With Welton (1991, 1987b) and Collins (1992, 1991), Brookfield (1989, p. 160) decries the absence of philosophical and political debate in contemporary North American adult education. He attributes its dearth to the technicist, professional discourse that now constitutes modern adult education practice, noting that "it is as if the search for academic respectability and the quest for professional identity have effectively depoliticized the field," creating, in the process, a "service-oriented rationale." While the technicist conception of adult education views the task of adult educators to be one of the effective and efficient transmission of knowledge and skills, Brookfield (1985, p. 284) argues that it is more properly

> that of encouraging adults to perceive the relative, contextual nature of previously unquestioned givens. Additionally, the educator should assist the adult to reflect on the manner in which values, beliefs and behaviors previously deemed unchallengeable can be critically analyzed. Through presenting alternative ways of interpreting and creating a world to adults, the educator fosters a willingness to consider alternative ways of living.

Welton (1991, 1987b), Collins (1992, 1991), and Brookfield (1989, 1985) share what Wilson (1991) describes as a "radical revisionist perspective" of adult education. At the root of this perspective lies a critique of the establishment's monolithic, technicist conception of adult education practice, a critique increasingly reflected in the adult education literature.[3] Cunningham (1989, p. 40), a staunch advocate of ethi-cally committed, anti-technicist adult education, voices a major con-cern of many of these remonstrators when she despairs that "the adult education literature has been reduced to describing the technology of adult education, in which 'means' have been elaborated into 'ends'. Thus the practitioner and graduate student alike have defined them-selves by an ahistorical technology."

I want to suggest that the emasculated conception of adult educa-tion practice that Cunningham (1989) and others reject is the product of a distinctively modern way of thinking that has systematically reduced the rich and varied realm of human experience to an impoverished and homogeneous sphere of empirically verifiable "facts." The sociologist Max Weber (1979), in a speech delivered at Munich University in 1918, referred to this denaturing process as the "disenchantment of the world." Weber borrowed this term from Friedrich Schiller to character-ize the distinctively modern process of "rationalization": the urge to displace indistinct and enigmatic ideas with those that reflect "system-atic coherence" and "naturalistic consistency."

## THE TECHNICIZATION OF ADULT EDUCATION

For many years, no clear and distinct idea of adult education practice existed in North America. In 1929, Lindeman, for instance, notes that "there was no such common term of currency as 'adult education' until after the late [1914–1919] war" (1929b, p. 29). The concept, "adult education," was used to refer to practices that were often anomalous, obscure, esoteric, ambiguous, eclectic, paradoxical, and even contra-dictory but practices, nonetheless, that constituted the lived educational experiences of adults. Adult education, Schied (1993, p. 7) notes,

> did not usually take place in places given over for one purpose. Rather it happened within the framework of cultural activities, events, and non-educational institutions. This education was not "rationally" designed with specific objectives and measurable out-comes but was often temporary, sometimes haphazard, and often transitory.

The concept, "adult education," then, despite its seemingly cryptic and amorphous nature, adequately captured the multiplicities of lived experience, referring to many different practices that were often peculiar to a particular context, practices that often changed from day to day and place to place. As such, those who employed the concept made no pretension to offer a systematic and exhaustive account of adult education practice, fully cognizant of the fact that the range of experiences to which it referred was constantly shifting and evolving. This rather nebulous concept, despite its equivocal nature, remained unproblematic until after the end of World War II when a number of likeminded adult educators decided to seek professional status for themselves and establish adult education as an academic discipline.[4]

Taylor (1987, p. 4) describes the years that immediately followed the end of World War II as "the heyday of logical empiricism." During this period, scientific thought equated the nonquantifiable with the meaningless; therefore, any concept that could not be exhaustively described in an empirically verifiable observation language was relegated to the realm of the fictional.[5] Then, as now, to be professional meant to have legitimacy, to have legitimacy meant to be admitted to the halls of the academy, to be admitted to the academy meant to be scientific, to be scientific meant to be meaningful, and to be meaningful meant to be quantifiable.

Prior to the advent of World War II, adult education practices in North America were many and varied.[6] The development of knowledge and practices tended to be specific to the interests of individual educators working in particular contexts with particular groups of learners.[7] During this period, the move to institutionalize adult education was in its germinal stage. Those adult educators who had gained access to the academy had yet to define an object of study, a body of knowledge, and a range of practices that would legitimate adult education as a science, to constitute what Foucault (1972) terms a "discursive formation." Their task was not an easy one, however, for as Welton (1991, p. 6) points out: "competing discourses jostle and struggle with one another over the control of the constituting process"; consequently, those who sought professional status had to subjugate "alternative knowledge forms," delegitimate them, and cast them "outside the arbitrarily delineated field" they were struggling to construct.

During this same period, however, political and philosophical issues remained of prime concern to other adult educators. Eduard Lindeman (1961, pp. 80–82), for instance, writing in 1926, bemoaned the effects of "an age of specialization" that "reduces citizenship to a false logical base," warning us that "when the function of citizenship loses its creativeness it also loses its meaning." To those who prescribed the further technicization and depoliticization of the United States, he cautioned that "Mussolini . . . found more parallels for fascism in the United States than anywhere else in the world. Our men of affairs discover that they can swim easily and comfortably in the waters of fascism—over there."

An emergent adult education establishment struggled, nonetheless, to legitimize a body of knowledge, a range of practices, and a lexicon of concepts—to constitute a *scientific* discursive field. This involved establishing an official discourse that excluded "whole areas of knowledge through a series of demarcations whilst . . . seeking to secure knowledge through methodological rules" (Frisby, 1976, p. xii). In the process, all "other" adult education discourses were delegitimated and relegated to the margins. In this manner, dissent was "discredited and delegitimized even before it was spoken—by the very absoluteness of the dominant syndrome, the universalism of its proclaimed ambitions and the completeness of its domination" (Bauman, 1992a, p. xiv). Consequently, only those practices that were amenable to scientific study

> were awarded the title of "adult education," all "others," practices that were not quantifiable, objective, or universalizable were deemed illegitimate and banished to the margins of the field. All modes of inquiry and forms of knowledge "other" than those of science were likewise dismissed in the establishment's drive to construct a body of knowledge distinctive to the field. All instructional methods and communicative processes "other" than those that maximized the effectiveness and efficiency of the adult learning process were likewise dismissed in the establishment's quest for control. (Briton and Plumb, 1993b, p. 55)

Newly construed and defined as a *positive* practice—as a *discipline* that progresses unerringly from indubitable facts through the rigorous application of unequivocable rules—professional adult education was able to accommodate the systematizing impulses of the workplace, the scientific demands of the academy, and the utopian, individualistic desires of the adult learner much more effectively. The role adult education played in the modernization[8] process was a far from insignificant one:

> The socialization of the worker to conditions of capitalist production entails the social control of physical and mental powers on a very broad basis. Education, training, persuasion, the mobilization of certain social sentiments (the work ethic, company loyalty, national or local pride) and psychological propensities (the search for identity through work, individual initiative, or social solidarity) all play a role and are plainly mixed in with the formation of dominant ideologies cultivated by the mass media, religious and educational institutions, the various arms of the state apparatus, and asserted by simple articulation of their experience on the part of those who do the work. (Harvey, 1989, p. 124)

In constructing a technicist discursive field that articulated with the dominant modernist discourses, a nascent adult education establishment succeeded in excluding all other "competing discursive fields vying for control of the field" (Welton, 1991, p. 26) and securing control of this emergent discipline-in-the-making.

Having established itself, the adult education orthodoxy consolidated its position by tailoring its discourse to meet the needs of the economic, academic, and social realms. To meet the requirements of the economic sphere, it attuned its discourse to Fordist mass production technologies and scientific management techniques. In the academic sphere, it defined a complete register of concepts, constructed an exclusive range of practices, and amassed a body of empirical-analytic knowledge, facilitating the development of a more exacting object of study.[9] In the social sphere, it adapted its concepts and practices to accommodate the ideology of the individual, endorsing psychologistic theories of learning and autonomous learning processes. Such actions prompted the emergence of the modern practice of adult education, a discursive field that draws on the science of behaviorism, argues for the distinctive nature of the adult learner, posits concepts like "self-directed" and "goal-oriented" learning, and promotes "contractual" learning processes and "facilitated" learning practices (Briton and Plumb, 1993b).

Law and Rubenson (1988, p. 232) contend that "Malcolm Knowles' *The modern practice of adult education*," is an exemplar of the professional discourse that dominated this period. Knowles, they argue, captured a sentiment that emerged within American adult education in the late 1950s and early 1960s and which came to frame much of the subsequent debate about the field's claim to a distinctive status. His concept of "andragogy" centred the identity of adult education on the discrete characteristics of adults as learners and thereby focussed attention almost exclusively on psychological and developmental considerations.

While Law and Rubenson are aware that "Knowles' model has never been accepted uncritically," they point out that many adult educators have embraced Knowles' andragogical model because of the distinctive status it affords adult education. They note, for instance, how "Darkenwald and Merriam (1982, p. 11) observe, 'there seems to be increasing agreement that the maturity of the adult learner and the needs and problems of adulthood are what give adult education its special quality'."

During the 1960s and 1970s, the adult education establishment focused on securing its place within the academy. It began in earnest to promote the field, expand graduate programs, organize conferences, form associations, and standardize curricula. By monopolizing the organs of public discourse, the establishment fortified its discursive boundaries against critical incursion. Brookfield, Wilson (1991, pp. 8–9) observes, "pinpoints 1964 as an intellectual watershed," referring us to Brookfield's (1989, p. 160) observation that "with the appearance in 1964 of the Commission of Professors of Adult Education's first important professional publication—*Adult Education: Outlines of an Emerging Field of University Study*—the movement towards greater professionalization and academic respectability gained momentum." In an aside, Wilson remarks of the aforementioned publication that even "the title is indicative of the change in perspective."

Marcuse (1964, pp. 12–13) relates the infatuation with technique and quantification that characterizes the 1950s and 1960s "to a development in scientific method: operationalism in the physical, behaviorism in the social sciences. The common feature is a total empiricism in the treatment of concepts; their meaning is restricted to the representation of particular operations and behavior."[10] Offering an analysis of the concept of "length," Marcuse outlines what operationalism entails:

We evidently know what we mean by length if we can tell what the length of any and every object is, and for the physicist nothing more is required. To find the length of an object, we have to perform certain physical operations. The concept of length is therefore fixed when the operations by which length is measured are fixed; that is, the concept of length involves as much and nothing more than the set of operations by which length is determined. In general, we mean by any concept nothing more than a set of operations; *the concept is synonymous with the corresponding set of operations.*

What is of particular concern to Marcuse is the fact that operationalism "involves much more than a mere restriction of the sense in which we understand 'concept'": it demands "a far-reaching change in all our habits of thought, in that we shall no longer permit ourselves to use as tools in our thinking concepts of which we cannot give an adequate account in terms of operations."

Nonetheless, the postwar intellectual community, greatly impressed with operationalism's positive contribution to the natural sciences, demanded equally rigorous concepts in *all* domains of inquiry. What often goes unheeded, however, is the fact that behind this drive to operationalize lies the *assumption* that inconsistency and contradiction—the twin perils of scientific inquiry—are epistemological phenomena, pitfalls of the intellect that can, and must, be avoided through diligent, disciplined thinking. The protests of those who argued that some concepts, especially those that express complex relations in the social realm, are necessarily murky and imprecise because the reality that spawns them is inconsistent and riddled with contradictions were simply dismissed, being incommensurable with logical empiricism's positivist thesis. One such protester, Theodor Adorno, for instance, remarks of the pre-eminent logical empiricist Karl Popper that "a problem is for Popper something basically epistemological and for me rather something practical, in the final instance *entirely a problematic condition of the world*" (Adorno, 1976, p. 129, emphasis added).

The implications of operationalism for adult education were significant. Once operationalized, the concept "adult education" took on not so much a whole new meaning as a partial, restricted one. This, in fact, was inevitable, for as Frisby (1976, p. xii) observes, "the sceptical or critical motive" in this positivist doctrine

seeks to exclude whole areas of knowledge through a series of demarcations whilst its affirmative impulse seeks to secure knowledge through methodological rules. This contrast between critical enlightenment and the defence of a restrictive theory of science has been a permanent feature of positivism's history.

Consequently, many practices that clearly involved the education of adults no longer corresponded to the set of operations that *defined* "adult education." The concept, then, became the measure of reality, rather than reality being the measure of the concept. This subjugation of practice to theory prompted Marcuse (1964, pp. 13–14) to conclude that "many of the most seriously troublesome concepts are being 'eliminated' by showing that no adequate account of them in terms of operations or behavior can be given"; this tendency, he warns, "serves to coordinate ideas and goals with those exacted by the prevailing system, to enclose them in the system, and to repel those which are irreconcilable with the system." Twenty-five years later, Collins (1991, p. 5) attests to the system's success, noting that "the obsession with methodology and technique has become so embedded in adult education practice and research that many practitioners are no longer able to recognize the way it controls and shapes adult learning activities." In *The Illusion of Technique*, Barrett (1979, p. 25) describes how the modern world secretly nourishes

> a fascination with technique itself. The publishing market is regularly flooded with "how to" manuals of all kinds. We turn to books to learn how to make love, and in consequence sex comes to be thought of as mainly a technique. Treatises on mental health appear that carry with them their own built-in little self-help kit of psychotherapy. All of this would be comic if it weren't so pathetic—and ultimately dangerous. This worship of technique is in fact more childish than the worship of machines. You have only to find the right method, the definitive procedure, and all problems in life must inevitably yield before it.

## UNDOING THE MODERN SUBJECT

Such forebodings support my own contention that the only way adult educators can even begin to question this distinctively modern "obsession with methodology and technique" (Collins, 1991, p. 5), a fixation that threatens to strip adult education and many other cultural practices of all qualities that are not tangible and quantifiable, is to look *beyond* the narrow, technicist concepts that guide contemporary thinking and action. The problem I faced, however, was that after working long and hard to develop an outline that reflected this position, the logic of my argument evaporated each time I tried to capture my ideas on paper.

Stranded, frustrated, and considerably annoyed, I found myself asking why my task was turning out to be so difficult. After all, I had talked about and discussed why it is important to carefully consider the moral and political consequences of the narrowly defined ideas that inform contemporary thinking and action many times. What I needed, I told myself, was a sounder structure to separate and delineate my thoughts. But every outline I drafted forced me to exclude points I wanted to, needed to, include. Once again, I was left angry and frustrated as all my attempts to construct an argument to justify my belief that adult educators should give serious consideration to the fundamental ideas that shape their thinking and guide their actions failed.

I *knew* the points I wanted to discuss were important, I *knew* they were all related in significant ways, and I *knew* they were worthy of being developed, but I just couldn't seem to capture that understanding. When I considered any one of the points I wanted to make, I sensed a logic that pulled me from that idea to another. Then, after considering that idea, I was lead to another, or sometimes I was lead back to my original thought to consider it anew, only to find that my understanding of it had been transformed. But what was it that led me from the first idea to the second and then back to the first? This was the reasoning, the relations between and among my thoughts, that I felt I had to be able to justify according to a logic that would be clear to *everyone*—an unimpeachable reason.

Then suddenly it occurred to me that this was one of the modern obsessions I was struggling to argue *against*. The idea that an objective standard of knowledge can be used to judge the validity of any claim to truth is one of the central tenets of logical empiricism, a doctrine I found myself *unconsciously* struggling to comply with even though I *consciously* oppose it. In trying to *clarify* my ideas, I was trying to *systematize* and *reduce* them to a degree of "objectivity" that I wanted to argue was a myth. That I had simply assumed that my scholarship was questionable if I couldn't make those relations *clear* and *distinct*, that is, unimpeachable or self-evidently true, is an indication of how strongly my consciousness, my very subjectivity, has been shaped by the model of understanding that dominates Western thought. This model, or theory, of understanding that posits a "natural" breach between the knower and the known, between the subject and the object, between the conceptual and the real, is the progenitor of the modern notion of self. This distinctively modern concept of the subject as detached and distinct from a world of "objects" is the condition for the possibility of the modern obsession with technique, for as Barrett (1979, p. 26) points out: "technique in its strictly technological sense" always involves

> two factors. (1) There must be a clear and distinct separation of the subjective and objective components in any situation in order for us to take rational hold of a problem. (2) The objective problem, thus isolated, is to be dealt with by a logical procedure that seeks to resolve it into a finite number of steps or operations that makes the obsession with technique possible.

This modern model of understanding, a model that now pervades Western culture, was the very model I was struggling to develop arguments against, yet my own subjectivity has been shaped by this model to such an extent that I was inadvertently formulating my arguments against it *within* the parameters of that very way of thinking.

It was then that I realized that my *understanding* of the relations among my ideas was, indeed, *my* understanding and that it was justifiable, not in terms of an immutable standard, whether external or internal, but in terms of my own intimate connectedness to the world my ideas disclosed. With this model of understanding in mind, I remembered how I had returned to books that I'd read months, weeks, or even days earlier only to find that the ideas and relations among ideas that I'd underlined so diligently—that I might return to the Truth—had no longer seemed significant. Why did I underline this? Why did I think this was important? Why did I feel this was relevant? These were the kinds of questions that, so often, I'd found myself asking. I remembered how, often, I'd found myself drawn to other passages, other sections of text that I'd disregarded as unimportant, only to find them pregnant with meaning. My understanding of what I'd read, I realized, had changed. I had been assuming that to be valid, my understanding had to be *static*, expressible in terms of general laws that anyone and everyone could apply to verify my claims to truth. This was when it occurred to me that the logic my inquiry *must* conform to is that of *my* understanding; otherwise, it would simply be a pretension to be something that it never can be—a "definitive," "objective," "value-free" description of a "petrified" world that differs significantly from my own experience of it. To proceed otherwise would be to endorse a model of understanding that I strongly oppose.

As I reflected on how my understanding actually progressed, I realized that it was my understanding of *all* my concepts that led me to relate one concept to another and then another. This progression, however, was not linear but dialogical, proceeding through an interplay of ideas, through a dialectical exchange that began with my struggle to understand a single concept in the light of my understanding of *all* of my ideas. After considering that first concept, however, my understanding was transformed, and it was this transformed understanding that lead me to consider the next idea, allowing me to envisage a relation that simply hadn't occurred to me before.

My problems had begun, I realized, when I *unconsciously* tried to match the *fluid* logic of my understanding to the *static* logic of the dominant model of knowledge. I had *assumed* that, to be valid, my understanding had to be "definitive," that it had to be an understanding that had *always existed*, an understanding just waiting to be *found*. Consequently, I had also assumed that my logic, to be valid, had to correspond to an unimpeachable logic that held for all people, in all places, at all times. While I *consciously* oppose this model of understanding, I had struggled, *unconsciously*, to conform to its standards. It wasn't until I became conscious of the imperative that was thwarting my progress that I was able to proceed, realizing that while my understanding is informed by all my ideas, as well a number of emotions, memories, hopes, fears, and experiences that may well serve to distort my thinking, there is, in fact, nothing that can be appealed to that will *prove* my understanding to be True. I had been laboring under the ancient belief that if I couldn't *prove* that my understanding was True, it was necessarily flawed.

It was at this point that I remembered the passage from Hegel's *Phenomenology of Spirit* that appears at the beginning of this chapter. I had been immobilized, I realized, by "the fear of falling into error," forgetting that "this fear presupposes something, *indeed a great deal, as truth*" (Hegel, 1974, p. 45, emphasis added). What I had been trying to do, *unconsciously*, was to translate a dynamic process of understanding into a single, static moment of Truth, something that is impossible to do because my understanding and all of the concepts that constitute my understanding are transformed whenever I consider a new idea. The only way to *define* this dynamic process would be to *freeze* or operationalize it at some point in the process, to *kill* it by excluding everything of which I could not be *certain.*

The logic that this work must conform to, then, is dialectical, a logic that proceeds from my own limited, finite understanding—warts and all—a logic implicit to my understanding that evaporated when I tried to express it in terms of a *universal, abiding* logic. It is a logic that does not try to capture "definitive" concepts or the "real" relations that exist between concepts because it recognizes that a single "snapshot" is a misrepresentation of the dynamic process that constitutes understanding. The justifications I offer for these claims will not be "objective," but they will be logical, rational, and reasonable, as logical, rational, and reasonable as we can get, I will argue.

## AN OUTLINE OF SORTS

The "outline" I now propose for myself is as follows: first, I will situate myself in the social and historical context that has shaped the understanding I have today; next, I will introduce the ideas and the thesis I want to pursue; then, I will proceed to justify my understanding of these ideas and the relations that I hold to exist among them. This is not, however, to sanction unbridled speculation, spontaneous leaps of faith, and a disregard for scholarship. The justifications that will be offered to support my understanding will have to be, if they are to be convincing, clearly explicated, reasonable, and believable, and this is where scholarship is essential. It is one thing to have a clear understanding of something and another to communicate that understanding clearly and convincingly. This process of inquiry may, at times, seem to be tangential but it will become plain, I hope, that it is a truer reflection of how thought actually proceeds. My justifications for this claim will constitute the work itself.

I can't say exactly how the work will end or how it will proceed— I can, of course, as I have in the past with smaller projects, pretend that I knew where I was going and how I would get there by writing an outline *afterwards.*[11] If I'm sensitive to my process of understanding, however, the concepts I consider will transform the understanding I now have, and this—I know from past experience—will lead me to explore concepts and relations among concepts that have not yet occurred to me. But this process will not and cannot be totally arbitrary: it will be guided by my belief that adult education is a cultural practice with moral and political implications that reach far beyond the classroom; by my belief that adult educators must give serious consideration to the moral and political implications of the theories and methodologies they choose to inform their practice and research; by the ideas I choose to begin considering; by my interests, which are inextricably linked to my understanding; by my past experiences; by my expectations and the expectations others have of me; by my desire to finish this project and to move on to the next; by the scope and limitations of a work of this nature; by what I have written thus far, for I can afford neither the time nor the resources to begin anew, so there will be an interest to return to what I've already written; and, I am sure, by much much more of which I am not yet aware but of which I will become aware as this work progresses—if I am sensitive to *my* understanding.

This work, then, is not my understanding *about* my ideas, it is my understanding *of* my ideas, and it proceeds, from time to time, in the first person to remind me *not to generalize*. It is my understanding of why adult educators should reflect upon the fundamental ideas that inform their thinking and guide their actions and I share it with you not because it is a "definitive" account but that you may consider the worth of the arguments made herein. Since the critique I offer cannot be evaluated in terms of formal structures or "objective Truths," it must provide its own justification. The reasons for moving from one idea to the next will not be "objective," and you, the reader, will be the final judge of their worth. Could it proceed otherwise? Very probably if I chose to start from elsewhere. But this is secondary.

While this critique argues against the modern, emasculated concept of adult education that leads educators to seek increasingly scientific and technological solutions to very human problems, it also argues for a different way of understanding. By critiquing the model of understanding that dominates Western scientific thought, it argues for a different model of understanding, a model that proceeds according to its own logic, a model of understanding that transcends individuals but which can only be expressed by individual thinkers. I think convincing arguments have always proceeded according to this model of under-standing—dialogically—through interplay and open exchange. It is only afterward that we go back and "discover" the beaten trail of our thoughts and pretend it already existed and that we did not *create* it but *followed* it—to "justify," to "objectify" a personal argument and make it *everyone's*: the modern obsession to generalize. I am convinced, how-ever, that

> ultimately, man finds in things nothing but what he himself has imported into them: the finding is called science, the importing—art, religion, love, pride. Even if this should be a piece of childishness, one should carry on with both and be well disposed toward both—some should find; others *we* others!—should import. (Nietzsche, 1886, in Nietzsche, 1968, §606, pp. 327)

## KNOWLEDGE GUIDING INTERESTS

Many contemporary thinkers offer convincing arguments that *all* the theories we employ to investigate our relationships with one another and the world are formulated within a social nexus, a community of dis-course that is the product of a shared history, tradition, and language.[12] Consequently, if I am to understand more fully the attributes of my *self* and the *selves* of those adults I hope to enter into a relationship of learn-ing with, it is imperative that I examine the limits and functions of the theories that inform my practice as an adult educator within my com-munity of discourse. This critique is structured toward that end. It is not structured toward developing a "better," or "correct," theory of the self or adult education. I do not believe that there are theories that are intrin-sically True or false, or better or worse only that there are possibilities for many *different* theories, theories that reveal not Truth or falsity but the *interests*, *aims*, or *goals* of those who formulate them (Habermas, 1972; Fay, 1975; Namenwirth, 1986; Lather, 1986).

According to Reinharz, "interest-free knowledge is logically im-possible"; she suggests, therefore, that we should "feel free to substi-tute explicit interests for implicit ones" (cited in Lather, 1986, p. 63), encouraging us to openly acknowledge the interests that lead us to view the world as we do. Since I, too, prescribe such a course of action, it is only fitting that I identify the values that shape my own view of the world. I make no claim that my values are or should be universal; that is, interests that *every* adult educator should embrace at *all* times, in *all* locations. If at some time I were compelled to make a normative claim of this sort, it would be this: Adult educators *should* be aware of the interests that guide *their* practice and research. I say this because to fail or to refuse to become aware of the theory or system of beliefs that guides one's practice—recognizing that all action is guided by some systematized account of experience, whether explicit or implicit—is not to adopt a neutral position, but to support those systematized accounts of experience that serve to maintain the status quo.

I have given up the belief that I can be totally objective, free of bias, prejudice, fear, guilt, or the urge to control; this is true of my dealings with others as well as myself. Admittedly, there are many social scientists who believe a disposition of disinterest can be maintained; nonetheless, I support Namenwirth's (1986, p. 29) contention that many "scientists firmly believe that as long as they are not conscious of any bias or political agenda, they are neutral and objective, when in fact they are only unconscious." In opposition to those who promote the vision of the disinterested, unprejudiced, scientific observer, Gadamer (1976, p. 9) argues that

> prejudices are not necessarily unjustified and erroneous, so that they inevitably distort the truth. In fact, the historicity of our existence entails that prejudices, in the literal sense of the word, constitute the initial directedness of our whole ability to experience. Prejudices are biases of our openness to the world. They are simply conditions whereby we experience something—whereby what we encounter says something to us.

Gadamer's (1976) point is that the act of coming to know *always* involves prejudice; we cannot, in fact, come to know anything without making *some* assumptions. The challenge, then, is to become aware of the prejudices or prejudgments—assumptions and presuppositions—that inform how we come to know. Consequently, before I present the problem of this work and the manner in which I propose to deal with it, I want to identify some of the factors in my own life that have shaped *my* judgment, for as Hall (1991, p. 18) notes: "there's no enunciation without positionality. You have to position yourself somewhere in order to say anything at all."

I was born a white, male, Anglo-Saxon, Protestant of working-class—I use the term advisedly—parents in England and I have suffered the consequences and enjoyed the privileges of this heritage ever since. From the age of eleven years on, I attended a grammar school for boys, where concerns of gender and race were neither discussed nor acknowledged.[13] I emigrated to Canada eighteen years ago, but unlike many immigrants, I have been neither the victim of persecution nor racial or sexual discrimination. In Canada, I studied at a technical institute to become a licensed electrician and worked for several years in the construction industry, an industry known neither for its equitable conditions nor its tolerance of difference. During this time, I was a member of a labor union and served as a job steward and local union officer and president. Today, I am a husband, a father of three children, and an educator—by *choice*, as Gail, my wife, is wont to remind me. I have a tendency to avoid or attempt to resolve conflict, rather than accept it as a positive manifestation of difference; speak, rather than listen; and generalize, rather than deal with specific issues. I am interested in critical forms of pedagogy that seek to establish democracy in the learning environment and to expose and to eradicate inequitable and unjust, asymmetrical power relations.

I am not alone in thinking that sexist and racist language has played an important role in perpetuating many unjust and undemocratic conditions. For this reason, I make a concerted effort to use language that does not privilege any particular subject position in all of my writing. I have deliberately chosen *not* to "neuter" some of the citations I employ, however, since to do so would detract from their force or intent. With Sayer (1991, p. 5), I tend to agree that the very fact that nineteenth- and early twentieth-century authors tended "to universalize under the sign of the modern the social experience of men should . . . be highlighted, not swept under a unisex carpet." Since when such authors "say 'Man', that is precisely who they usually mean," it is pointless "to imagine this deficiency can be remedied by changing the gender of pronouns." To attempt to do so "is to efface even more thoroughly that world of feminine experience . . . so conspicuously neglected," and "it is also, of course, patronizing in the extreme." It is with these factors in mind that I present my thesis.

# 3

## *Facing the Dilemma*

> Only in so far as one is free from the
> power of institutions to determine and
> to disseminate ideas, and from the
> power of habit to make of culture a
> second nature, is one free to evaluate
> received opinions, and to obey the
> Socratic injunction to examine the life
> one is living in the midst of the *doxae*
> and to know the self the theory of
> whose limits and functions is among
> the *doxae*.
>
> —Wiseman, 1989, p. 4

### MORAL AND POLITICAL IMPLICATIONS

Should I, as an adult educator, be concerned to free myself from the power of the institutions and culture of contemporary Western society to the extent that I can "evaluate received opinions," examine the life I am "living in the midst of the *doxae*," and come to understand my own self, "the theory of which is among the *doxae*" (Wiseman, 1989, p. 4)? Viewing the task of adult educators to be simply one of facilitating the transmission of knowledge and skills, the adult education establishment would have us believe that adult educators need not concern themselves with questions of this nature. This, however, is to fail to recognize that adult education is a *cultural* practice with moral and political *consequences* that reach far beyond the walls of the classroom. The task I undertake, herein, is to show that adult educators are cultural workers as opposed to technicians and for this very reason, it is essential that they critically "evaluate received opinions," critically examine the life they are "living in the midst of the *doxae*," and come to understand their innermost selves, "the theory of whose limits and functions is among the *doxae*."

What is not readily apparent to many adult educators, however, is that in embracing a particular theory of how adults come to know, a theory or model of knowledge—something they *cannot* avoid doing as educators—they help to legitimate and to reproduce that model.[1] Often unwittingly, the model most adult educators adopt is that of the empirical-analytic tradition, a tradition comprised of a number of intimately related ideas, an alliance of beliefs, practices, doctrines, and customs that have been transmitted from generation to generation and which now articulate together to dominate Western thought. That the empirical-analytic tradition's theory of knowledge now pervades the modern practice of adult education is clear from Wilson's (1991) insightful analysis of the adult education handbooks published between 1934 and 1989.[2] This model of knowledge, however, is based on a distinctively modern *understanding* of what knowledge *is*, a model of understanding that lies at the very heart of the empirical-analytic tradition: an understanding that identifies knowledge with that which *is* apodictic, that which *is* irrefutable, that which *is* certain, that which *is* incontestable, that which *is* unimpeachable, etc.

This *understanding* of knowledge has permeated Western culture to such an extent that it is simply taken for granted that epistemologists—those whose object of study is knowledge—*must* proceed to develop their theories from this understanding of knowledge, an understanding that posits a realm of isolated, knowing *subjects* radically divorced from a world of discrete *objects*. What the epistemological community fails to recognize, however, is that epistemologists, who have set themselves the task of differentiating that which *claims* to be knowledge from that which *is* knowledge, are forced to *assume* what knowledge is *before* they can explain that which distinguishes it from all else. This, however, as Hegel noted in 1817, is to proceed under "the misconception of already knowing before you know—the error of refusing to enter the water until you have learnt how to swim" (Hegel, 1974, p. 147). While admitting that it is reasonable to want to subject our understanding to scrutiny, Hegel asks:

yet what is this scrutiny but *ipso facto* a cognition? So that what we want is to combine in our process of inquiry the action of the forms of thought with a criticism of them. The forms of thought must be studied in their essential nature and complete development: they are at once the object of research and the action of that object. Hence they examine themselves: in their own action they must determine their limits, and point out their defects.

Hegel, therefore, replaces epistemology's highly questionable conception of understanding with one he chooses to call "Dialectic," noting that, "we need only at the outset observe that instead of being brought to bear upon" our ideas "from without, it is immanent in their own action." This *indigenous* model of understanding reveals the implicit inadequacies of the *exogenous* model that informs the empirical-analytic tradition, a tradition that provides the institutions of the modern world, including mainstream adult education, with the fundamental axioms, rationale, and justification to pursue technical and scientific solutions to all of humanity's problems.

## KNOWLEDGE, VALUES, AND SCIENCE

In reference to the empirical-analytic tradition's understanding of knowledge, Taylor (1987, p. 466) remarks: "if I had to sum up this understanding in a single formula, it would be that knowledge is to be seen as correct representation of an independent reality." Taylor notes, however, that this understanding of knowledge "is bound up with very influential and often not fully articulated notions about science and about the nature of human agency," notions that serve to connect it "with certain central moral and spiritual ideas of the modern age." These ideas articulate with one another to form a hegemonic bloc, an alliance of ideas that adult educators help to legitimate and reproduce when they unquestioningly adopt the tradition's theory of knowledge.

As Darkenwald and Merriam (1982, p. 37) attest:

> many adult education practitioners engaged in the daily tasks of program planning, administration, or teaching have little time to reflect upon the meaning and direction of their activity. The educator is generally more concerned with skills than with principles, with means than with ends, with details than with the whole picture. Yet all practitioners make decisions and act in ways that presuppose certain val-

ues and beliefs. Whether or not it is articulated, a philosophical orientation underlies most [I would argue *all*] individual and institutional practices in adult education.

That adult educators tend to concern themselves with "skills," "means," and "details," rather than "principles," "ends," and "the whole picture" and are generally unaware of the moral and political consequences of their practice is, I want to suggest, because the "values and beliefs" they embrace, largely unconsciously, are those of the empirical-analytic tradition, a tradition that values "objectivity" and "disinterest" over all else, while arguing that "scientific knowledge," the *sine qua non* of objectivity and disinterest, "is, in itself, politically and morally neutral" (Keat, 1981, p. 2).

For a number of years, the empirical-analytic tradition's theory of knowledge—a model that has usurped the title of epistemology for itself—dominated Western thought. It was revered as the *foundational* enterprise of our scientific culture, as the manifestation of the ancient belief that *all* and *any* claim to truth can be verified by way of reference to an *unwavering* standard of knowledge. "Fifty years ago," Taylor (1987, pp. 464–465) notes, during its "heyday . . . , logical empiricism . . . was not only a powerful movement in philosophy but also immensely influential in social science." As such, epistemology was rejoicingly acknowledged as that which

> the positive sciences needed to complete them, . . . a rigorous discipline that could check the credentials of all truth claims. An alleged science could only be valid if its findings met this test; otherwise it rested on sand. Epistemology would ultimately make clear just what made knowledge claims valid, and what ultimate degree of validity they could lay claim to.

Taylor (1987, p. 465) reminds us, however, that while the earliest proponents of epistemology were well aware that their enterprise could not "be dependent on any of the empirical sciences, and this obviously on pain of a circularity that would sacrifice its foundational character," they invariably "took their cue from what they identified as the successful sciences of the day." Much of epistemology's force, in fact, derives from its close affinity with the empirical sciences that emerged during the sixteenth and seventeenth centuries. The modern notion of science that appeared soon after, the nomological- or hypothetico-deductive model—a conception of science that construes scientific practice in terms of a rigorous, rule-governed *method* adjudicated by empirically verifiable facts—is an amalgam of epistemology's formal, analytic reasoning and empirical science's experimental method. This model of science, Aronowitz (1988, p. 8) notes, "reduces [scientific practice] to two procedures: mathematical calculation and experimental validation/ falsification of results."

Having operationalized the concept of science, that is, having *reduced* scientific practice to its "essential" nature, this purportedly *exhaustive* model of science, proceeded to *steer* scientific practice, ineluctably, toward its ultimate goal: the total domination of nature. It was this startling reduction of science to a methodology and the remarkable subordination of practice to theory that led Nietzsche, in 1888, to conclude that "it is not the victory of science that distinguishes our nineteenth century, but the victory of scientific method over science" (Nietzsche, 1968, §466, p. 262). This immaculate model, nonetheless, became the cornerstone of the empirical-analytic tradition, a tradition with a long and venerable history that stretches from Descartes, through Locke, Hume, Kant, and Russell to Popper. Consequently, when criticisms of the epistemology that informed this sacrosanct model first emerged from outside of the empirical-analytic tradition, they were dismissed perfunctorily.

## THE HISTORICAL CRITIQUE OF SCIENTISM

It was not until certain historically minded scientists from *within* the empirical-analytic tradition—notably Kuhn (1970) and Feyerabend (1988), and to some degree Lakatos (1970)—challenged the tradition's *seamless* construal of scientific practice that the doubts outsiders had previously expressed about the omniscient enterprise of epistemology began to be taken seriously. It soon became difficult to deny that from a historical perspective, "neither our arts nor our sciences have characters fixed or continuous through time and social space," and that

> nature has ruptures in the theories that give it shape, discontinuities
> in its smooth working: Newtonian physics does not hold when the
> objects to which it is applied are moving at a speed approaching the

speed of light, and deterministic laws of physics do not hold true of quanta. (Wiseman, 1989, p. 16)

The historically minded scientists who challenged the scientific establishment, however, were branded apostates by the scientific community and subjected to a level of vitriolic and scathing criticism that far exceeded reasonable proportions.[3] This hostile and highly emotional reception, I want to suggest, was not due to their critique of epistemology, as such, but to what was perceived to be a threat to the tradition's whole network of ideas, of which epistemology, itself, forms only a small part.[4]

While most critiques of the modern conception of science from within the empirical-analytic tradition—with the exception of Feyerabend's (1988)—were, in fact, concerned almost exclusively with loosening epistemology's apodictic grip on the scientific imagination, they were construed by advocates of the tradition to be threats to the existing moral and political order. Such fears, as it happens, turned out not to be totally unfounded. In challenging the empirical-analytic tradition's pristine methodological model, these critics called into question the legitimacy of the West's social, educational, political, and economic institutions, institutions that had adopted, unreservedly, not only the tradition's impeccable methodology but also the values and beliefs implicit to its practice. This unmitigated faith in the tradition's scientific method Habermas (1972, p. 4) dubs *scientism*: "the conviction that we can no longer understand science as *one* form of knowledge, but rather must identify knowledge with science."

The empirical-analytic tradition, Taylor (1987, pp. 471–472) informs us, "is connected with some of the most important moral and spiritual ideas of our civilization—and also with some of the most controversial and questionable." These ideas—which Taylor suggests are more properly "anthropological beliefs" or "key theses about the nature of the human agent"—serve as the central tenets of modern Western society. That their veracity is largely unquestioned is because they are derivatives of the mode of understanding that dominates Western culture, that of the empirical-analytic tradition. Products of the same process of reductive naturalism that spawned the tradition's "flawless" methodological model, these fundamental ideas are the moral and spiritual consequences of the tradition's mode of thought, the unacknowledged *political* ends that serve to justify its *technicist* means. These largely unconscious ideas about the "essential nature" of the human subject are the empirical-analytic tradition's greatest strength, ideas whose constitutive role is often overlooked in the urgency to discredit its foundationalist epistemology and narrow, technicist construal of knowledge.

"It is safe to say," Taylor (1987, p. 473) contends, that epistemology's most insightful critics—who he suggests are Hegel, Heidegger, Merleau-Ponty, and Wittgenstein—"were largely motivated by a dislike of the moral and spiritual consequences" of the mode of thought that informs the empirical-analytic tradition; "the connection between the scientific and the moral," he notes, "is generally made more evident in their work than in that of mainstream supporters of the epistemological standpoint." These critics, Taylor points out,

> establish a new moral outlook through overturning the modern conception of knowledge. They do not just register their dissidence from the anthropological beliefs associated with this conception, *but show the foundations of these beliefs to be unsound, based as they are in an untenable construal of knowledge.* (emphasis added)

The task these theorists set themselves is one that others have since embraced: to convince those who unquestioningly accept the empirical-analytic tradition's narrow, technicist conception of knowledge that important aspects of life, of our "being-in-the-world" (Heidegger, 1962), cannot be accommodated within the tradition's denuded construal of experience. The problem is that while, "superficially, technology looks like the pure servant of freedom" because "by increasing our powers it multiplies our opportunities to be free," what is often overlooked is that

> in attaining those powers we could very well lose the direct and organic sense of our relatedness to nature that humankind once knew; or, in Heidegger's words, we could attain a mastery over beings but lose the sense of Being itself. We can thus imagine a technical society of the future that had conquered its material problems but was afflicted with a loss of meaning that its own technical thinking left it unable even to grasp. (Barrett, 1979, p. xx)

## SCIENCE AS IDEOLOGY

According to Barthes (1973), our most fundamental ideas about knowledge, nature, and even our own identity—Taylor's (1987) "anthropological beliefs"—constitute our culture's "myths"; that is, the stories "by which a culture explains or understands some aspect of reality or nature" (Fiske, 1992, p. 88). While primitive myths, Fiske notes, are about "life and death, men and gods, good and evil," the West's "sophisticated myths are about masculinity and femininity, about the family, about success, . . . and about science." Our ideas, then, are neither the "impressions" nor the "reflections" of an objective reality but linguistic constructs, shared *cultural* conceptions that emerge when the members of a community struggle to make sense of their lived experience.

The concept of *understanding*, then, the idea of how human beings come to know, is shaped, along with every other concept, by the aims or interests of the community in which it emerges. Consequently, since *all* our ideas are *always* shaped by the interests or values of the community in which we find ourselves, they can never be either value-free or objective. The question, then, becomes one of *how* and *why* proponents of the model of understanding that lies at the heart of the empirical-analytic tradition—the representational model of knowledge—a concept premised on the ideas of "value-freedom" and "objectivity," have been able to convince the vast majority of Westerners to unconsciously *value* the concepts of "value-freedom" and "objectivity" while consciously *denying* that very interest. A growing number of theorists now argue that *ideology* provides the answer to the first question, while *power and control* provide the answer to the second.

The Italian political theorist and activist Antonio Gramsci (1989) argues that many of our underlying interests go largely unrecognized because our cultural conceptions are not the product of *conscious* deliberation but of "common sense," of "the uncritical and largely *unconscious* way of perceiving and understanding the world that has become common in any given epoch" (Hoare and Smith, in Gramsci, 1989, p. 322, emphasis added). These conceptions, in fact, comprise "an 'anonymous ideology' penetrating every possible level of social life, inscribed in the most mundane of rituals, framing the most casual encounters" (Hebdige, 1979). As such, they provide the *ethos*, the ideological framework *within* which the members of a culture or community grapple to make sense of their lived experience, to become conscious of their relationship to one another and the world. It is the very ubiquity and transparency of these largely *unconscious* ideas that invests them with their tremendous power, power to shape even the consciousness of their progenitors.

While most adult educators are willing to concede that some of their ideas may well have been shaped by largely unconscious ideological forces, most believe that they need only *adjust* or *purge* those distorted ideas to ensure that they accurately "reflect" the real. Proponents of the empirical-analytic tradition suggest as much, arguing that we can *guarantee* that our concepts are free of cultural biases, of the prejudices of tradition and authority, if we *limit* the meaning we attribute to them to that which we can *publically* confirm: to that which we can empirically verify or analytically validate. One of the earliest proponents of this view in the field of adult education was E. L. Thorndike.

Thorndike, Wilson (1991, p. 16) contends, "the first to begin systematic studies of adult learning in the 1920s, was clearly linked to the logical-empiricist (empirical-analytic in Habermas' terms) research tradition with his focus on measuring adult intelligence . . . , [and] an interest in control based on empiric knowledge." Thorndike, in fact, was mesmerized by the reductive naturalism of the empirical-analytic tradition early in the century, predicting that

> a complete science of psychology would tell every fact about everyone's intellect and character and behavior, would tell the cause of every change in human nature, would tell the result which every educational force—every act of every person that changed any other or the agent himself would have. It would aid us to use human beings for the world's welfare with the same surety of the result that we now have when we use falling bodies or chemical elements. In proportion that we get such a science [*sic*], we shall become masters of our souls as we now are masters of heat and light. Progress toward such a science is being made. (Thorndike, 1910, cited in Kim, 1991, p. 70)

What educators such as Thorndike find so attractive about the empirical-analytic tradition is its appeal to the observable, to the quantifiable, to the *bare and indisputable facts*, to *common sense*. The tradition's notion of common sense, however, differs significantly from that of Gramsci's (1989), referring to purportedly apodictic concepts, to concepts untainted by historical and contextual biases, to "such 'first truths' as that there is an external world, that our minds are incorporeal, that we are capable of free agency" (Grave, 1967, p. 156). Grave notes of the seemingly indisputable "first truths" of common sense that

> first truths have characteristic marks: No attack upon them, and no attempt to prove them, can operate from premises that surpass them in clarity or evidence. They are, and always have been, acknowledged by the vast majority of mankind. Those who imagine they reject them act like other men in conformity with them.

Hebdige (1979, p. 11), however, wary of such universalistic claims, warns us that it is "at the level of 'normal common sense' that ideological frames of reference are most firmly sedimented and most effective, because it is here that their ideological nature is most effectively concealed." One might ask of Grave (1967), for instance, where "the vast majority of mankind" who acknowledge the truths of common sense *actually* reside, or who they *actually* are. Such universalizing turns of phrase carry distinctly Eurocentric overtones, imposing upon all of humankind distinctively modern European values and beliefs, including what McLaren (1993, p. 121) describes as "the magnificent Enlightenment swindle of the autonomous, stable and self-contained ego that is supposed to be able to act independently of its own history, its own cultural and linguistic situatedness, and free from inscriptions in the discourses of, among others, gender, race and class." In an illuminating *exposé* of the notion of common sense that informs the empirical-analytic tradition, Hall (cited in Hebdige, 1979, p. 11) cautions that

> it is precisely its "spontaneous" quality, its transparency, its "naturalness," its refusal to be made to examine the premises on which it is founded, its resistance to change or correction, its effect of constant recognition, and the close circle in which it moves which makes common sense, at one and the same time, "spontaneous," ideological and *unconscious*. You cannot learn, through common sense, *how things are*: you can only discover *where they fit* into the existing scheme of things. In this way, its very taken-for-grantedness is what establishes it as a medium in which its own premises and presuppositions are being rendered *invisible* by its apparent transparency.

Convinced of the insidious nature of common sense, Hebdige concludes that "since ideology saturates everyday discourse in the form of common sense, it cannot be bracketed off from everyday life as a self-

contained set of 'political opinions' or 'biased views'" (p. 12). Hebdige, then, with some reservations, offers confirmation of what Althusser (1979, p. 233) has long contended: that "ideology has very little to
do with 'consciousness'."[5]

## THE ROLE OF IDEOLOGICAL STRUCTURES

Ideology, Althusser (1979, pp. 231–235) declares, "is a system (with its
own logic and rigor) of representations (images, myths, ideas or concepts, depending on the case) endowed with a historical existence and
role within a given society"; as such, it is *an organic part of every
social totality.*" Althusser insists that ideology is *indispensable in any
society if men are to be formed, transformed, and equipped to respond
to the demands of their conditions of existence*"; it is "a structure essential to the historical life of societies," but a structure that "has very little
to do with 'consciousness'," since it is "in truth, . . . profoundly *unconscious.*"

It may be somewhat of a challenge for some adult educators, impli-
cated as they are in the everyday realm of common sense, to envisage
how ideological structures, that is, the largely unconscious beliefs that
form the basis not only of our cultural institutions but also our very
identities, shape our ideas about our selves and the world to such an
extent that we actively seek to mold our selves and the world to conform to our distorted understanding of it. While Althusser (1979, p.
233) is singular in his insistence that these structures are real, that is,
that "they are *perceived-accepted-suffered cultural objects* [emphasis
added] and [that] they act functionally on men via a process that
escapes them," his language is abstract and his meaning oftentimes elu-
sive. Hebdige (1979, pp. 12–13), however, suggests that we can gain a
better understanding of just how these structures shape our consciousness and how we come to unconsciously reproduce them in material
form if we draw upon an analogy. The analogy he offers is that of an
everyday physical structure, an institute of education:

> Most modern institutes of education, despite the apparent neutrality
> of the materials from which they are constructed (red brick, white
> tile, etc.) carry within themselves implicit ideological assumptions
> which are literally structured into the architecture itself. The catego-
> rization of knowledge into arts and sciences is reproduced in the fac-

ulty system which houses different disciplines in different buildings, and most colleges maintain the traditional divisions by devoting a separate floor to each subject. Moreover, the hierarchical relationship between teacher and taught is inscribed in the very lay-out of the lecture theatre where the seating arrangements—benches rising in tiers before a raised lectern—dictate the flow of information and serve to "naturalize" professorial authority. Thus a whole range of decisions about what is and what is not possible within education have been made, however unconsciously, before the content of individual courses is even decided.

Consequently, *predetermined* decisions shape not only *what* is taught but also *how* it is taught. The institute's very buildings, Hebdige notes, serve "to literally *reproduce* in concrete terms prevailing (ideological) notions about what education *is*." As a result, "the educational structure, which can, of course, be altered, is placed beyond question and appears to us as a 'given' (i.e. as immutable)."[6] From Hebdige's example, then, we can see how "the frames of our thinking have been translated into actual bricks and mortar."

"It is customary," Althusser notes, "to suggest ideology belongs to the region of 'consciousness'," but he warns us that "we must not be misled by this appellation" (1979, p. 232–233), for ideology entails not just what "we commonly call religious ideology, ethical ideology, legal ideology, political ideology, etc., so many 'world outlooks'," but also "the imaginary relationship of individuals to their *real* conditions of existence" (1992, p. 52, emphasis added). Althusser, then, does not deny the existence of an underlying reality, only our *conscious* access to it. The real, he argues, is such that our concepts of it are always over-determined by it, precluding the possibility of ever formulating an exhaustive account of the natural. Of Althusser's structuralism Geras (1987, P. 16) writes:

> Its chief target was empiricism, a view of cognition in which the knowing subject confronts the real object and uncovers its essence by abstraction and which seeks, from this assumption of thought's direct encounter with reality, of the subject's unmediated vision of the object, for external guarantees of knowledge's truth.

While the concepts and language Althusser uses to discuss ideology can be confusing to those unfamiliar with the Hegelian/Marxist tradition, the distinction he draws between *imagined* and *real* relations is an important one to grasp. By examining Kuhn's (1970) critique of the seamless construal of science that lends such great force to the empirical-analytic tradition more closely, I hope to cast more light on this crucial distinction for those more familiar with the concepts and language of the empirical-analytic tradition.

## ANOTHER IMAGE OF SCIENCE

In his seminal work, *The Structure of Scientific Revolutions*, Kuhn (1970) argues that a certain *ethos* underlies the practice of Western science, that the members of the Western scientific community—"normal science"—share an outlook or attitude toward the world, a perspective or "paradigm," that first took shape during the sixteenth and seventeenth centuries. While Kuhn's account of paradigms is not always clear, his historical analysis of the *practice* of Western science suggests that paradigms "may be prior to, more binding, and more complete than any set of rules for research that could be unequivocally abstracted from them" (p. 46). In a somewhat more telling account, Patton (1975, p. 9), extrapolating from Kuhn's rather circumspect notion, describes a paradigm as

> a world view, a general perspective, a way of breaking down the complexity of the real world. As such, paradigms are deeply embedded in the socialization of adherents and practitioners telling them what is important, what is legitimate, what is reasonable. Paradigms are normative; they tell the practitioner what to do without the necessity of long existential or epistemological considerations.

Kuhn (1970) employs an historicized vision of scientific practice to challenge the empirical-analytic tradition's ahistorical, seamless conception of science, to confront what Gouldner (1971, p. 17) describes as "the search for convergences with and in the past," a search wherein the tradition "calls, seeks to reveal a tacit consensus of great minds and, by showing this, to lend credence to the conclusions that they are held to have converged upon unwittingly. *Convergence thus becomes a rhetoric, a way of persuading men to accept certain views*" (emphasis added). That this model of science fails to capture essential aspects of scientific practice is clear not only to Kuhn but also to Feyerabend (1988, p. 14), who notes that

> one of the most striking features of recent discussions in the history and philosophy of science is the realization that events and developments, such as the invention of atomism in antiquity, the Copernican Revolution, the rise of modern atomism (kinetic theory; dispersion theory; stereochemistry; quantum theory), the gradual emergence of the wave theory of light, occurred only because some thinker either *decided* not to be bound by certain "obvious" methodological rules, or because they *unwittingly broke* them.

In defense of his position, Kuhn proposes, instead of "the image of science by which we are now possessed" (p. 1), an "image" that he feels better reflects the unexpurgated history of *actual* scientific inquiry.

The model Kuhn (1970) offers can be characterized in terms of a series of stages. In its infancy, science, Kuhn argues, proceeds haphazardly, practiced by "schools and subschools" of inquirers who follow their own guiding principles; this is science's *preparadigmatic* stage. After a while, however, a paradigm emerges to guide scientific practice—"universally recognized scientific achievements that for a time provide model problems and solutions to a community of practitioners" (p. viii); this is science's *normal* stage. "Normal science," Kuhn contends, "means research firmly based upon one or more past scientific achievements, achievements that some particular scientific community acknowledges for a time as supplying the foundation for its further practice" (p. 10). The practice of "normal science," however, leads to the discovery of anomalies that cannot be solved within the existing paradigm, precipitating a "crisis" and the development of alternative paradigms. This marks the emergence of science's *extraordinary* stage: when "an anomaly comes to seem more than just another puzzle of normal science, the transition to crisis and to extraordinary science has begun" (p. 82). Finally, an alternative paradigm emerges that can explain what the decadent paradigm cannot, and while scientists are at first reluctant to "renounce the paradigm that has led them into crisis" (p. 77), "crisis simultaneously loosens the stereotypes and provides the incremental data necessary for a fundamental paradigm shift" (p. 89). Kuhn is convinced that "the resulting transition to a new paradigm is scientific revolution" (p. 90), an event that he likens to a political revolution because like the choice between competing political institutions, that between competing paradigms proves to be a choice between incompatible modes of community life. Because it has that character, the choice is not and cannot be determined merely by the evaluative procedures characteristic of normal science, for these depend in part upon a particular paradigm, and that paradigm is at issue. When paradigms enter, as they must, into a debate about paradigm choice, their role is necessarily circular. Each group uses its own paradigm to argue in that paradigm's defense. ( p. 94)

Kuhn's (1970) historical analysis of scientific practice, then, gives the lie to the empirical-analytic tradition's sacrosanct incremental methodological model, revealing science's actual development to be one of ruptures and revolutions, rather than incremental evolutionary change. Perhaps more importantly, however, Kuhn's analysis exposes science's *cultural* core, pointing out that the kind of logic that determines theory choice during times of crisis is not a disinterested, universal, objective one but a value-laden, historically specific, intersubjective one. Kuhn is convinced this is the case because "the type of argumentation that takes place at times of scientific crises and revolutions can be resolved neither by an appeal to the canons of deductive logic or proof nor by any straightforward appeal to observation, verification, confirmation, or falsification" (p. 52). Kuhn is insistent that during times of scientific crisis, reasons do not function as rules that can be applied disinterestedly but

as values and that they can thus be differently applied, individually and collectively, by men who concur in honoring them. If two men disagree, for example, about the relative fruitfulness of their theories, or if they agree about that but disagree about the relative importance of fruitfulness and, say, scope in reaching a choice, neither can be convicted of a mistake. Nor is either being unscientific. There is no neutral algorithm for theory-choice, no systematic decision procedure which, properly applied, must lead each individual in the group to the same decision. (pp. 199–200)

## SCIENCE AS RATIONAL DISCOURSE

While Kuhn (1970) contends that many of modern science's most significant discoveries cannot be accounted for in terms of the empirical-analytic model, he recognizes that most scientists simply take it for granted that this model offers an exhaustive account of scientific practice, due to epistemology's apodictic grip on the scientific mind. The empirical-analytic conception of science *shapes* the consciousness of those within the scientific community to such a degree that scientists always seek to explain their discoveries in terms of this model. This "dominant, hegemonic ideology," Bottomore (1987, p. 202) notes, functions "to provide a more coherent and systematic world view which not only influences the mass of the population but serves as a principle of organization of social institutions." Feyerabend (1988, pp. 16–17) offers a typically acerbic account of the scientific establishment's hegemony, arguing that

> just as a well-trained pet will obey his master no matter how great the confusion in which he finds himself, and no matter how urgent the need to adopt new patterns of behavior, so in the very same way a well-trained rationalist will obey the mental image of *his* master, he will conform to the standards of argumentation he has learned, he will adhere to those standards no matter how great the confusion in which he finds himself, and he will be quite incapable of realizing that what he regards as the "voice of reason" is but a *causal after-effect* of the training he had received.

The flawless *appearance* of the empirical-analytic model of science, then, stems not from impeccable a priori reasoning and indisputable facts but from the empirical-analytic tradition's ability to *coerce* those within the scientific community into believing that new ideas that emerge during actual scientific practice *must* be explicable in terms of the tradition's sacrosanct methodology *before* they can be granted "scientific" status. As Aronowitz (1988, p. 8) notes: "modern science demarcates itself, not by reconstituting the object, but by defining rationality in a specific way." The problem, as Eisner (1983, p. 14) notes, is that when science is operationalized,

> when one defines research in a particular way and then defines competence in terms of the way research is defined, only competent researchers (i.e., those who do what is conventional) will have access to the pages of research journals. Assistant professors seeing other lights, but seeking tenure as well, are in a bit of a bind.

The issue Eisner (1983) identifies is typically the problem that confronts new faculty who oppose the adult education establishment's technicist conception of the field. It is, however, also a problem that adult education graduate students who reject the narrow, denatured, operationalized model of adult education must confront. The situation within the academy is such that it is extremely difficult for graduate students to even conceive of adult education practices other than those prescribed by the orthodoxy. While mention is made of "alternative" and "other" ways of practicing adult education, the vast majority of study is devoted to familiarizing students with the register of *positive* concepts, range of *technicist* practices, and body of *empirical-analytic* knowledge that now constitutes the field; that is, with the *professional* discourse that dominates modern adult education practice. The establishment's ideological technicist discourse, then, does not deny the existence of nontechnical "discursive practices" (Foucault, 1972), but such practices are always represented as "other" than or "deviant" from the "norm."

Inevitably, faculty members are well versed in only one of the many discursive fields that actually constitute adult education practice—the technicist professional discourse of the establishment. Consequently, faced with the arduous task of having to complete a research project or thesis, many graduate students feel compelled to formulate a research question and embrace a methodology that will not take an inordinate amount of time and effort to defend. To stay within the boundaries of the dominant professional discourse is to minimize the number of questions that will be asked and significantly limit the justifications that will be called for. While resistance is possible, it comes at a price—a price many cannot afford or are unwilling to pay. To choose a discourse other than the professional discourse of the establishment to conduct research is not simply to be different, it is, by default, to be "irrational." The establishment's technicist discourse is now so firmly ensconced as the "rational," all "other" discourses, by virtue of their difference, are deemed "irrational." This means that those who wish to pursue research within the context of an "irrational" discourse must be prepared to defend and justify that discourse at every turn. The cost of resistance can be high.

In the scientific community, Feyerabend (1988, p. 11), a fervent critic of orthodox scientific discourse, has been ridiculed and ostracized for his "irrationality." Feyerabend argues that actual scientific practice involves much that the empirical-analytic tradition would have us believe is "irrational" and that these delegitimated but important aspects of practice can only be accommodated within a much broader conception of science than that of the scientific establishment. In a typically trenchant statement, he notes that

> the history of science . . . does not consist of facts and conclusions drawn from facts. It also contains ideas, interpretations of facts, problems created by conflicting interpretations, mistakes, and so on. On closer analysis we find that science knows no "bare facts" at all but that the "facts" that enter our knowledge are already viewed in a certain way and are, therefore, essentially ideational. This being the case, the history of science will be as complex, chaotic, full of mistakes and entertaining as the ideas it contains, and these ideas in turn will be as complex, chaotic, full of mistakes, and entertaining as are the minds of those who invented them. Conversely, a little brain washing will go a long way in making the history of science duller, simpler, more uniform, more "objective" and more readily accessible to treatment by strict and unchangeable rules.

## ILLUSIONARY ALLUSIONS

Having examined Kuhn's (1970) critique of the concept of scientific practice that the empirical-analytic tradition *imagines* to be real, we can now substitute Kuhn's terms for Althusser's (1992) to understand better the latter's distinction between *real* and *imagined* relations. While Althusser speaks of "institutions" or "ideological apparatuses" rather than "communities" or "normal science," of "structures" rather than "paradigms," and of "imagined relations" rather than "theories," his argument mirrors that of Kuhn's—up to a point. Structures, Althusser contends, which are *always already* within institutions, determine how members of those institutions come to *imagine* their relation to the world. Much like paradigms, then, structures function to determine "what is important, what is legitimate, what is reasonable. . . . [Both] are normative; they tell the practitioner what to do without the necessity of long existential or epistemological considerations" (Patton, 1975, p. 9). Althusser, however, carries his critique one step further than Kuhn.

    While Kuhn (1970), much to the chagrin of the empirical-analytic tradition, points out that the tradition's conception of scientific practice—the hypothetico-deductive paradigm—functions in the same manner as what "we commonly call religious ideology, ethical ideology, legal ideology, political ideology, etc., so many 'world outlooks'" (Althusser, 1992, p. 52), he fails to recognize that ideas, even when they are stripped of epistemology's foundationalist pretensions, will still be the product of ideological forces. This is because ideas are never *unmediated* re-presentations of the real as Kuhn and other adherents of the empirical-analytic tradition take them to be, but images of "the imaginary relationship of individuals to their real conditions of existence" (Althusser, 1992, p. 52). Consequently, while Kuhn's critique exposes the ideological nature of paradigms by drawing attention to the fact that "these 'world outlooks' are largely imaginary, i.e. do not 'correspond to reality'," he is led to believe that while "they constitute an illusion, . . . they do make an allusion to reality, . . . that they need only be 'interpreted' to discover the reality of the world behind their imaginary representation of that world" (Althusser, 1992, p. 52).

Kuhn, for instance, describes his critique as "an attempt to show that existing theories of rationality are *not quite right* and that we must *readjust* them to explain why science works as it does" (cited in Bernstein, 1985, p. 59, emphasis added). This is to suggest that while paradigms serve to distort our ideas of the world, *somehow*, we can "compensate for" or "get behind" those distortions to an undistorted or nonideological re-presentation of reality. But as Althusser (1992) notes, our ideas are never simply re-presentations or pristine images of the real, they express, rather, "the *imaginary* relationship of individuals to their real conditions of existence" (p. 52, emphasis added). This second moment of ideology, a distinctively Marxian moment that entails the shaping of consciousness, itself, eludes Kuhn, whose analysis of ideology stops at the level of consciousness, at the level of representation.[7] Kuhn and other adherents of the empirical-analytic tradition simply fail to recognize that

> only an ideological world outlook could have imagined societies *without ideology* and accepted the utopian idea of a world in which ideology . . . would disappear without trace, to be replaced by *science*. (Althusser, 1977, p. 232)

Kuhn (1970) accepts, unquestioningly, that the empirical-analytic tradition's understanding of knowledge somehow provides those who embrace it with a portal to reality, with an *unmediated* grasp of the natural, with a guarantee that their mental images of the natural, once stripped of epistemological distortions, will be accurate "reflections" of the real. This, however, neglects to take into consideration *material* distortions that are the product of the material conditions, of the cultural context in which human beings *become conscious* of themselves and their world. Our ideas, the very concepts through which we become conscious of our selves and the world, are not *unmediated* images of the natural but concepts that are *always already structured* by the conventions, traditions, and language of the world in which we find ourselves (Barthes, 1973). Consequently, the nexus of ideas that constitute the empirical-analytic tradition—including its "key theses about the nature of the human agent" (Taylor, 1987, p. 471), the founding principles of the West's ethico-political order—are far from indubitable, *appearances* notwithstanding.

## IMAGINING THE REAL

In *The German Ideology*, Marx and Engels argue that since ideas are, necessarily, the product of lived experience, they are *always* conditioned by the material conditions in which the thinkers of those ideas—concrete, living and breathing individuals of a particular time and place—find themselves. The "ruling ideas" of any epoch, Marx and Engels argue, "are nothing more than the ideal expression of the dominant material relations, the dominant material relations grasped as ideas; hence of the relations which make the one class the ruling one, therefore, the ideas of its dominance"; they continue:

> If now in considering the course of history we detach the ideas of the ruling class from the ruling class itself and attribute to them an independent existence, if we confine ourselves to saying that these or those ideas were dominant at a given time, without bothering ourselves about the conditions of production and the producers of these ideas, *if we thus ignore the individuals and world conditions which are the source of the ideas*, then we can say, for instance, that during the time the aristocracy was dominant, the concepts honour, loyalty, etc., were dominant, during the dominance of the bourgeoisie the concepts freedom, equality, etc. The ruling class itself on the whole imagines this to be so.

Once the ruling ideas have been separated from the ruling individuals and, above all, from the relations which result from a given
stage of the mode of production, and in this way the conclusion has
been reached that history is always under the sway of ideas, it is very
easy to abstract from these various ideas "the Idea," the thought, etc.,
as the dominant force in history, and thus to consider all these separate ideas and concepts as "forms of self-determination" of the Concept developing in history. *It follows then naturally, too, that all the
relations of men can be derived from the concept of man, man as conceived, the essence of man, Man.* (Marx, 1989, pp. 6–7, emphasis
added)

There can be little doubt that the "ruling ideas" of the current epoch
are those of the empirical-analytic tradition, or more properly, of the
philosophers of the tradition—that whole nexus of ideas that provides
the ends for and serves as the basis of Western culture. For as Marx
noted in 1842, "philosophers do not spring up like mushrooms out of
the ground; *they are products of their time, of their nation,* whose most
subtle, valuable and invisible juices flow in the ideas of philosophy"
(Marx, 1989, p. 5, emphasis added). "Consciousness," Marx and
Engels contend, "can never be anything else than conscious being, and
the being of men is their actual life-process"; consequently, in contrast
to ideologies that descend "from heaven to earth," they propose "a matter of ascending from earth to heaven. That is to say, not of setting out
from what men say, imagine, conceive, in order to arrive at men in the
flesh; *but setting out from real, active men, and on the basis of their real
life-process demonstrating the development of the ideological reflexes
and echoes of this life-process*" (Marx, 1989, p. 5, emphasis added).
Adherents of the empirical-analytic tradition, Kuhn (1970) included,
fail to recognize that when material conditions are inequitable, the
ideas those conditions engender are distorted or "inverted," "as in a
*camera obscura*" (Marx, 1989, p. 5).[8] Such ideas are distorted because
they are shaped by the interests of those in power, rather than the interests of humanity in general, being "nothing more than the ideal expression of the dominant material relations, the dominant material relations
grasped as ideas; hence of the relations which make the one class the
ruling one, therefore, the ideas of dominance" (Marx, 1989, p. 6).

Taylor (1987, pp. 471–472) argues that the dominant ideas of the
current epoch, the commonsense assumptions of the empirical-analytic

tradition, ideas about the nature of knowledge, the world, and human beings—"anthropological beliefs" that serve as the basis of Western civilization—are, indeed, distortions that result from the tradition's "inverted" model of understanding:

> The first is the picture of the subject as ideally disengaged, that is, as free and rational to the extent that he has fully distinguished himself from his natural and social worlds, so that his identity is no longer to be defined in terms of what lies outside him in these worlds. The second, which flows from this, is a punctual view of the self, ideally ready qua free and rational to treat these worlds—and even some of the features of his own character—instrumentally, as subject to change and reordering in order the better to secure the welfare of himself and other like subjects. The third is the social consequence of the first two: an atomistic construal of society constituted by, or ultimately to be explained in terms of, individual purposes.

## THE ADULT EDUCATOR'S DILEMMA

That these fundamental beliefs are now considered to be *natural* human traits is beyond question, and that these ideas have far reaching moral and political implications can hardly be denied; the question remains, however, of whether the empirical-analytic tradition's *ideas* about human nature and the natural order, once freed from the distortive influence of the modern scientific paradigm are, in fact, *actual* representations of the real or *imagined* ones. *If* these ideas accurately reflect our reality, *if* we are, indeed, *naturally* self-conscious subjects that are divorced from the world and those around us, *if* we are subjects who *naturally* know a world of objects through our internal representations of them, *if* we are *naturally* self-responsible agents, *if* the universe does conform, *naturally*, to universal laws, *then* the empirical-analytic tradition's world view would be of great use to help us structure an ethico-political order to meet our *natural* needs.

However, *if* the empirical-analytic tradition's world view does not accurately reflect our reality and it "is inherently repressive, and contributes to the maintenance of a form of society in which science is one of the resources employed for the domination of one class by another, and in which the possibilities for a radical transformation towards a more rational society are blocked and concealed," and *if* "the attempt to formulate universal laws governing social phenomena leads to the misrepresentation as eternal or natural of what should instead be seen as historically specific and alterable" (Keat, 1981, p. 2), *then* the ideas of the empirical-analytic tradition clearly would be far from neutral and objective and obviously should not be used to shape an ethico-political order that would perpetuate this form of domination.

For many adult educators the thought of having to deal with questions such as these is daunting. That adult education involves more than simply the transmission of knowledge and skills and that adult educators are cultural workers who wittingly or unwittingly legitimate and reproduce the most fundamental beliefs of their culture should, however, now be clear. There are, in fact, a number of adult educators who have always construed adult education as a cultural practice, recognizing that the understanding of knowledge they adopt, the theory of knowledge they embrace, and the ideas about science and human nature that they accept have moral and political consequences that reach far beyond the classroom. It is imperative, however, that *all* adult educators recognize that they are intimately involved in a *cultural* practice that can buttress or undermine the existing moral and political order.

Contrary to popular belief, then, it is impossible to be an adult educator and be apolitical. When we choose to adopt or simply assume the seemingly "neutral" and "objective" methodology of the empirical-analytic world view to inform our practice and research, we commit ourselves to an understanding of knowledge, science, and human nature that a growing number of thinkers are calling into question. To embrace a particular model of understanding—wittingly or unwittingly—is to endorse certain fundamental assumptions that serve, or seek to serve, as the basis for an existing, or prescribed, moral and political order. Like it or not, choose we must, for to refuse to do so *consciously* is to support the existing ethico-political order *unconsciously*. Is the existing ethico-political order that is based on the empirical-analytic perspective neutral and objective or manipulative and oppressive? How might one tell?

The challenge to those who strongly oppose the moral and political consequences of the empirical-analytic tradition's "anthropological beliefs," Baynes, Bohman, and McCarthy (1987, pp. 460–461) note, has been to reveal "the untenability of the picture of the self as disengaged and disembodied, punctual and atomistic, related to the natural and social worlds, and even to parts of the self, only as objects of disinterested knowledge and instrumental control," and to show rather that "we are first and foremost embodied agents in a natural and social world," that "our propositional knowledge of this world is grounded in our dealings with it and [that] there can be no question of totally objectifying the prior grasp we have of it as agents within it." This entails, above all else, showing that the empirical-analytic tradition's "naturalism derives its plausibility from a background of 'strong evaluations' and 'distinctions of worth' and that the hermeneutic standpoint can provide a better account of these than competing standpoints." How might such a demonstration begin? Perhaps with an examination of the empirical-analytic tradition's emergence with the advent of modernity and the dawning of the European Enlightenment.

# 4

# Enlightenment and Modernity

> REASON WITHOUT PREJUDICE, knowledge without proscription, and an empirical mode of inquiry are the fundamental principles of the Enlightenment. Behind such a definition, however, lies a barely disguised utopianism that makes it easier to understand the enduring strength of the Enlightenment and the status of empirical science as one of its dominant paradigms. Kant's judgment that the Enlightenment marked humanity's release from a state of immaturity illustrates a pervasive attitude within it . . . : the recovery of nerve . . . , the attempt to regain control over both fate and the environment by making reason the ruler in human affairs.
>
> —Langford, 1992, p. 24

## THE MODERN DISPOSITION

Not until modernity did the West's "anthropological beliefs . . . , beliefs in the disengaged subject, the punctual self, and described atomism" (Taylor, 1987, p. 476) fully emerge. These beliefs are the product of a certain disposition toward the world, of an *ethos* that surfaced in the seventeenth century, of what Foucault (1984, p. 39) describes as an "attitude of modernity." This disposition, "often characterized in terms

57

of consciousness of the discontinuity of time: a break with tradition, a feeling of novelty, of vertigo in the face of the passing moment," emerged only after the Renaissance began to give way to the Age of Reason, when "what is thought of as *modern* society took shape in the seventeenth century in the northwest corner of the European system of societies, in Great Britain, Holland, and France" (Parsons and Platt, 1973, p. 1). During this period, intellectual opinion in Europe began to drift,

> from an admiring preoccupation with the history, literature, and language of the ancient world, especially Rome, and from Christian theology and ritual, logical formality, scholastic thought, and authoritarianism, towards a confidence in the superiority of modern novelties and modern powers, reasonable religion and secular values, personal expression and plain style, a critical appeal to reason and the rule of sensible evidence, and individualistic, egalitarian freedom of practice, thought, and judgement. (Nidditch, 1975, p. xvii)

"Common to the drifts and tendencies," Wiseman (1989, p. 3) notes, "is an attitude toward the past, an attitude that stems from the belief that the past serves the present," an attitude that gives rise to the notion "that modernity is a seeing-through."[1] It was Baudelaire, however—in 1863—who first formulated the notion of modernity as a *seeing-through*.

"Modernity," Baudelaire (1964, p. 13) declared, "is the transient, the fleeting, the contingent; it is the one half of art, the other being the eternal and the immutable." For Baudelaire, modernity is an attitude that seeks to grasp the essential nature of the present—the *eternal* and *immutable*—only to transform it and experience it anew—the *transient* and the *fleeting*. As such, modernity is a *seeing-through* to "the essential character of the accidental" (Klee, cited in Harvey, 1989, p. 12). Modernity, then, "is an exercise in which extreme attention to what is real is confronted with the practice of a liberty that simultaneously respects this reality and violates it" (Foucault, 1984, p. 41).

Baudelaire's characterization of modernity as the ephemeral, the transient, the contingent, and the fleeting has won favor with many contemporary students of modernity. Berman (1982, p. 15), for instance, writes that there is a mode of vital experience—experience of space and time, of the self and others, of life's possibilities and perils—that is shared by men and women all over the world today. I will call this body of experience "modernity." To be modern is to find ourselves in an environment that promises adventure, power, joy, growth, transformation of ourselves and the world—and, at the same time, that threatens to destroy everything we have, everything we know, everything we are. Modern environments and experiences cut across all boundaries of geography and ethnicity, of class and nationality, of religion and ideology; in this sense modernity can be said to unite all mankind. But it is a paradoxical unity, a unity of disunity; it pours us all into a maelstrom of perpetual disintegration and renewal, of struggle and contradiction, of ambiguity and anguish. To be modern is to be part of a universe in which, as Marx said, "all that is solid melts into air."

"This overwhelming sense of fragmentation, ephemerality, and chaotic change," Harvey (1989, p. 11) notes, is "echoed by Frisby . . . who in a study of three modern thinkers—Simmel, Kracauer, and Benjamin—emphasizes that 'their central concern was with a distinctive experience of time, space and causality as transitory, fleeting, and fortuitous and arbitrary'."

The attitude of modernity," writes Foucault (1984, p. 41), "the high value of the present is indissociable from a desperate eagerness to imagine it, to imagine it otherwise than it is, and to transform it not by destroying it but by grasping it in what it is." But it is only after "a world-historical process of crystallization that transpires over the course of the 15th, 16th, and 17th centuries or the 'early modern period'," according to Wolin (1985, p. 9), that modernity achieves this, its "definitive form." "The modern age is," Barrett (1979, pp. 196–197) declares, "the flowering of enlightenment out of the narrow other-worldliness of the Middle Ages," reminding us that "three great events had combined to usher in this period—the Renaissance, the Reformation, and the development of science." It was the Renaissance and Reformation, Habermas (1987, p. 286) argues, that unleashed "the cognitive potentials contained in the traditions of Christianity and of ancient Rome and Greece," potentials "previously worked up only by cultural elites in monastic orders and universities." The Reformation, for instance, "abolished the barriers between clergy, religious orders, and laity and set the impulses of religious ethics of conviction free to shape profane realms of action," while "the humanism of the Renaissance

made the Roman-Greek heritage accessible to the science, jurispru-
dence, and art that were emancipating from the church."

Spurred by the emergent *ethos* of modernity, profoundly influenced
by events of the Reformation and Renaissance, and notably impressed
by remarkable advances in the realms of arithmetic, geometry, astron-
omy, and physics during the sixteenth and seventeenth centuries—the
culmination of which was the publication of Newton's *Principia*, in
1687—a coterie of European thinkers, the *philosophes* (radical intellectuals, such as, Condorcet, D' Holbach, Turgot, and Voltaire), formulated and began to popularize the idea of "progress," the belief that
human beings could and should be the masters of their own destiny,
rather than the servants of authority and the minions of tradition. "Modern civilization, they argued, represented a definite advance in the history of humanity" (Seidman, 1989, p. 2).

The *philosophes*, Copleston (1985, p. 35) notes, were

> a kind of international and cosmopolitan-minded set of thinkers and
> writers who were united at any rate in their hostility, which showed
> itself in varying degrees according to circumstances, to ecclesiastical
> and political authoritarianism and to what they regarded as obscu-
> rantism and tyranny. And they looked on philosophy as an instrument
> of liberation, enlightenment and social and political progress. They
> were, in short, rationalists more or less in the modern sense, free-
> thinkers with a profound confidence in the power of reason to pro-
> mote the betterment of man and society and with a belief in the dele-
> terious effects of ecclesiastical and political absolutism.

According to Seidman (1989, p. 2), these first critics of Europe's *ancien
régimes* were convinced that "as the rationality embodied in science,
law, moral philosophy and art penetrated into daily life, social progress
would be an inevitable outcome." Convinced that "dogmatic traditions
function, in effect, as ideologies reifying and legitimating the existing
hierarchical social arrangements," the *philosophes* attributed the
absence of "freedom and happiness" in Europe (in particular, France)
to the "dominance of false beliefs." Perpetuated "by religious and metaphysical dogmas," such beliefs served to keep "individuals in a state of
ignorance and oppression," they argued. Consequently, "in the face of
an unfreedom rooted in ignorance," they appealed to "experience or to

empirical observations in order to discredit dogmatic beliefs and norms."

Ignorance, then, was thought to be the great oppressor of humanity, yet to escape its thralldom human beings, the *philosophes* argued, need only *will* themselves to understand their predicament. Hence Kant (1983, pp. 41–42), in 1784, declared: "*Sapere Aude!*[2] 'Have courage to use your own understanding!'—that is the motto of enlightenment." Individuals, however, in order to exercise their reason, their distinctively human capacity to understand, needed to be free, for "nothing is required for this enlightenment," Kant argues, "except *freedom.*" Reason and freedom, then, were inextricably linked for Enlightenment thinkers, who were convinced that once reason was freed to investigate the human predicament, it would divest nature of its mystery, expose the fallacious grounds of superstition, deliver individuals from the arbitrary powers of despotic rulers, and reveal the path to an equitable and just society.

Anderson (1991, p. 36) describes the *philosophes*' struggle as one against "three fundamental cultural conceptions, all of great antiquity," long taken-for-granted suppositions that held an "axiomatic grip on men's minds":

> the first of these was the idea that a particular script-language [Church Latin] offered privileged access to ontological truth, precisely because it was an inseparable part of that truth. . . . Second was the belief that society was naturally organized around and under high centres—monarchs who were persons apart from other human beings and who ruled by some form of cosmological (divine) dispensation. . . . Third was a conception of temporality in which cosmology and history were indistinguishable, the origins of the world and of men essentially identical.

"Combined, these ideas," Anderson argues, had "rooted human lives firmly in the very nature of things, giving certain meaning to the everyday fatalities of existence (above all death, loss, and servitude) and offering, in various ways, redemption from them." But convincing the populace of a civilization premised on regress, the power of the supernatural, and traditional values to break with convention was no easy task. For this very reason, eighteenth-century reformers "were attracted to the natural scientific method," convinced that "its proven and celebrated success in assisting man to understand and better control the physical universe" could be turned to developing "a science of humanity through which reason (the use of mind) would be supplemented by experience (the use of the senses, especially observation)" (Hearn, 1985, p. 10). Jürgen Habermas (1987)—arguably modernity's leading proponent and critic—conceives of the task Enlightenment radicals set themselves as a "project," a project that spawned the empirical-analytic tradition—the Project of Modernity.

## THE APOTHEOSIS OF REASON

The Project of Modernity, Wolin (1985, p. 10) notes, prompted an "irrevocable transition," a transition from all premodern forms of association—"based on *cosmological* world-views . . . characterized by the predominance of a single, monolithic value-system which pervades and structures its various partial subsystems"—to a modern form of association—based on "*de-centered* or *differentiated* world-views" characterized by the emergence of "individually functioning 'value-spheres'," that are "allowed to pursue their own inherent 'inner logics'." This resulted in the emergence of natural philosophy, political philosophy, and aesthetics as *autonomous* value-spheres, realms of endeavor that "no longer need a priori invoke the authority of an antecedent and determinative cosmological standpoint to legitimate themselves." While this project demanded great intellectual effort, Enlightenment thinkers devoted to the task of advancing civilization by liberating Europe's populace from oppressive traditions and beliefs willingly accepted the challenge to develop *sciences*—exacting and systematized accounts—of the emergent realms of nature, morality, and art. For those involved in the project,

> the scientific domination of nature promised freedom from scarcity, want, and the arbitrariness of natural calamity. The development of rational forms of social organization and rational modes of thought promised liberation from the irrationalities of myth, religion, superstition, release from the arbitrary use of power as well as from the dark side of our own human natures. Only through such a project could the universal, eternal, and the immutable qualities of all humanity be revealed. (Harvey, 1989, p. 12)

Wishing to discredit conventional wisdom and promote the Project of Modernity, a project "founded on the Enlightenment's belief in progress, the belief that all societies can and should be changed by the power of Reason and according to universally valid value criteria" (Richters, 1988, p. 611), the *philosophes* evangelically touted "the power of reason to yield truths about the human, natural, and social worlds," arguing that reason "provides a vantage point from which to critically reflect upon reified social conventions and to achieve some release from their constraining power"; reason's "ultimate aim," they argued, "was to advance individual freedom by promoting critical self-reflection" (Seidman, 1989, p. 2–3).

Reason, the *philosophes* maintained, because its authority stemmed not from tradition or faith but from "its absolute universality and necessity," from the fact that its "claims were not limited to a particular context or set of conditions but applied equally to all men at all times" (Richters, 1988, p. 611), should be the measure of *all* things. Arguing that "church, state, social, and economic class, superstition, ignorance, prejudice, poverty, and vice all seemed to work together to impede the proper functioning of Reason" (Brinton, 1967, p. 520), eighteenth-century reformers demanded a break with history and tradition and the demystification and desacrilization of all forms of knowledge and social organization, dismissing traditional forms of reasoning as either scholastic fabrications or priestly inventions, as devices that served to hold human beings in ignorance.

Certain that reason, once unimpeded, had the potential not only to foster progress but also to (re)discover Nature—humankind's natural state, beneath the corrupting forms of religion, culture, convention, and improperly organized sense experiences—Enlightenment thinkers rejected all metaphysical notions of good and evil, along with all other aspects of the supernatural, in favor of "an optimistic, this-worldly belief in the power of human beings, brought up rationally from infancy on as nature meant them to be, to achieve steady and unlimited progress toward material comfort and spiritual happiness for all men on this earth" (Brinton, 1967, p. 521). So strong was the allure of nature that the latter half of the eighteenth century witnessed the birth of "primitivism," the doctrine that human beings had once existed in a free, natural state. It is interesting to note, Brinton comments, that while "the state of nature is what we would now call a myth," during the eighteenth century it served as a form of "propaganda for a new order," along with that other "very popular political concept, the 'social contract'," the mechanism that "brought 'natural' ethics into practical politics as the natural rights of man."

Modernity, then, dealt tradition and authority shattering blows. For many, "the evermore evident insufficiency of unreflexive custom as a guarantee of social existence was perceived as the withdrawal of God from the world," and since "God could no longer be addressed, conversed with or induced to intervene . . . , humankind was now left to its own resources—above all it had to build up its existence using the most perfect of God's gifts, reason" (Bauman, 1992b, p. 2). The transition from sacred to secular, then, was accomplished through the unhindered practice of reason,

> by making good choices, only good choices and ever better choices. Making good choices itself turned into the *telos*; there could be no other end to human existence, since any other end would put a limit to reason's power. The sole purpose of reason was its own application, its rule, its mastery. Reason's mastery over humans as persons was the only meaning of the emancipation of humanity as a species; the only sensible model for humanity reaching finally its destination, its *telos*. The species' eternal self-perfection, called *progress*, required now that everything else is temporal, transient and disposable. (Bauman, 1992b, p. 4)

Convinced that "true humanity was embodied in the cosmopolitan individual and in universal human nature, not in mere customs and contingencies" (Richters, 1988, p. 611), Enlightenment thinkers pursued a dramatic break with the past, a break that would permit the untramelled use of reason, the unmitigated conquest of nature, the unhindered pursuit of progress, and the subsequent liberation and contentment of humankind. Hardly surprisingly, then, eighteenth-century radicals embraced modernity's maelstrom of change, its transitoriness, its fleeting and fragmentary nature, and welcomed it as a necessary precondition for the realization of their project.

## THE BIRTH OF THE MODERN SUBJECT

It was in this context, Taylor (1987, pp. 472–476) argues, that the beliefs that form the basis of the empirical-analytic tradition—those of

"the disengaged subject, the punctual self, and described atomism"—
first emerged to challenge those of Europe's *ancien régimes*:

> The first notion emerges originally in classical duallism [Descarte's
> *Cogito*], where the subject withdraws even from his own body, which
> he is able to look on as an object; but it continues beyond the demise
> of this dualism in the contemporary demand for neutral, objectifying
> science of human life and action. The second originates in the ideals
> of the government and reform of the self that have such an important
> place in the seventeenth century and of which Locke develops an
> influential version; it continues today in the tremendous force that
> instrumental reason and engineering models have in our social pol-
> icy, medicine, psychiatry, politics, and so on. The third first takes
> shape in seventeenth-century social contract theories, but continues
> not only in other contemporary successors but also in many of the
> assumptions of contemporary liberalism and mainstream social sci-
> ence.

Long since "naturalized," these beliefs have dropped from consciousness and now serve to shape our thinking about the world, leading us, a
growing number of thinkers contend, to accept and participate in forms
of practice and governance that contribute to our own domination.
These beliefs constitute the core of the "modern disengaged identity," a
notion of self "which centers everything on the subject and sets up a
'quite unreal model of clarity and control', that is behind the hegemony,
in the modern period, of atomistic, utilitarian, instrumentalist, and for-
malist modes of conceptualizing human thought and action" (Baynes et
al., 1987, pp. 460–461). This distinctively modern mode of thinking,
however, "in illuminating the obscurantism of the old order, . . . cast
upon society a light which blinded men and women to the murky
sources of this clarity" (Eagleton, 1991, p. 64).

While the Enlightenment's "rejection of metaphysics" did divest
nature of its mystery and subject it to humanity's whims, it did not,
Phelan (1989, p. 21) contends, lead "to the revelation and celebration
of the play of power that had been lurking behind old ideals or ration-
ales"; nor did it lead "to the justification of new power, but rather to the
veiling of power in a new language," for "as religion and metaphysics
become suspect, science becomes the new basis for ontology and tele-
ology, and so for social power." Foster (1992, p. 160) is convinced that
this masking of power is no accident, linking "the program of the

Enlightenment" to the interests of an emergent economic force—capitalism.

The Enlightenment's program, Foster (1992, pp. 160–161) argues, is "the broadest example of bourgeois ideology," an ideology of "the natural rights of man, the sovereignty of the people and of the republic, of a public sphere 'open' to all interests and a state 'above' all conflicts." While admitting that "this project of *universal* representation was conceived in resistance to the *special* interests of the aristocracy, monarchy and church," he notes how "its very liberatory program—to naturalize, rationalize, universalize—has come to be seen as the ideological operation par excellence." Horkheimer and Adorno (1978, in Foster 1992) for instance, contend that under the auspices of the bourgeoisie,

> the Enlightenment has become its own dark other, its own grotesque myth; the role of reason encompasses the capitalist domination of nature, the imperialist eradication of the other, the fascist regression into the irrational (and now the potential extinction of us all).

In fact, a growing number of thinkers are now questioning the foundations of the Enlightenment's project, especially those that cast human beings as, first and foremost, self-conscious, detached rational agents. While "common sense . . . assumes that the nature of human 'being' is given in some way—that it exists *prior* to language," and that "within this framework, the human individual is conceived as a unified centre of control from which meaning emanates" (Easthope and McGowan, 1992, p. 67), a different idea of the subject is emerging to challenge this perspective. This idea, Easthope and McGowan argue,

> decentres the individual by problematizing the simplistic relationship between language and the individual which common sense presumes. It replaces human nature with concepts of history, society and culture as determining factors in the *construction* of individual identity, and destabilizes the coherence of that identity by making it an *effect* rather than simply an origin of linguistic practice. Instead of being confirmed by recourse to a universalizing principle, "humanity" (which then confirms the world which surrounds it), the subject is seen as *made* and so open to transformation. In other words, the theory of the subject proposes a notion of identity as precariously constituted in the discourses of the social whereby it is both determined

and regulated by the forces of power inherent in a given social formation, but capable also of undermining them.

If self-consciousness does, indeed, arise out of communicative practices, practices that entail the use of language in a sociohistorical setting, it would clearly be a mistake to conceive of humans as *essentially* self-conscious individuals, since self-consciousness and personal identity would be derivatives of a sociolinguistic context. While it is difficult to imagine how our very identities might be the product of forces other than those of nature, a growing body of evidence suggests that some of our most fundamental beliefs about human nature may be mistaken. It is worthwhile, then, turning to four separate accounts—those of Marx, Nietzsche, Elias, and Heidegger—that attribute the emergence of the modern notion of the subject—as "something essential, substantial, unitary, fixed, and fundamentally unchanging" (Kellner, 1992, p. 142)—to forces other than those of nature.

## FOUR ACCOUNTS OF SUBJECTIVITY

The notion that individuals are "naturally" divorced from their fellows has been challenged by a number of socially conscious thinkers. Many of these theorists attribute the modern individual's sense of estrangement not to natural tendencies but to social, economic, and political forces. While such theorists seek to capture the distinction between premodern and modern forms of association in various ways, all share the view that the modern notion of self was the product of sociohistorical forces.[3] Karl Marx, undoubtedly one of the most influential of such social theorists, attributes the appearance of the modern alienated self to economic and political forces that began to emerge in the sixteenth century.

According to Sayer (1991, p. 12), Marx is unrelenting "in his insistence that what makes modernity modern is, first and foremost, capitalism itself." Capital, for Marx, is "the demiurge of the modern world . . . 'the general light tingeing all other colours and modifying them in its specific quality', 'a special ether determining the specific gravity of everything found in it', 'the economic power that dominates everything in modern society'. Capitalism *is* modernity and modernity capitalism." It was, then, according to Marx (1983a, p. 204), the emergence of the capitalist mode of production in Britain that created "modern bourgeois society" and initiated "the epoch of the bourgeoise"—a dramatically new mode of life that differed radically from all earlier forms of association.

As opposed to custom and tradition, the mark of all earlier epochs, constant change became the hallmark of the modern era. All traditional forms of production and association that hindered the process of modernization were swept aside. Writing in 1848, Marx and his associate Frederick Engels offer a sobering and poignant account of the forces that were reconstituting the very fabric of nineteenth-century Europe, forces that served not only to thrust Europe's communities into the modern era but also to obscure the relations of dependence that bound community members together:

> Constant revolutionizing of production, uninterrupted disturbance of all social conditions, everlasting uncertainty and agitation distinguish the *bourgeois* epoch from all earlier ones. All fixed, fast frozen relations, with their train of ancient and venerable prejudices and opinions, are swept away, all new-formed ones become antiquated before they can ossify. All that is solid melts into air, all that is holy is profaned. (Marx, 1983a, p. 207).

An emergent *bourgeoisie*, Marx and Engels argue, promptly initiated a conscious political struggle to dismantle the medieval institutions that impeded increased productivity in Britain's fledgling manufacturing industries (Larrain, 1987). By challenging and overturning feudal restrictions, such as, those on free trade, the personal freedom of workers, the practices of guilds, and the restriction of usury, the *bourgeoisie* initiated a capitalist revolution that spawned an era of unprecedented economic growth. In less than a century, radical political reforms "freed" rural populations from their feudal ties with the land, and fundamental economic reforms that fostered mass production technologies rapidly transformed Britain from an agrarian into an industrial society. The result was massive social upheaval as rural populations, stripped of the means of providing their own sustenance—the land—converged on the industrialized centres to "freely" exchange their only remaining possession—their labor—for wages. This maelstrom of political, economic, and social change transformed, dramatically, not only how people worked but also how they viewed their relations to one another.

Prior to the advent of capitalism and the onset of industrialization, political power and rights of possession were identified with individuals—the feudal king, prince, or lord—and all individuals in a given community were bound together through readily identifiable relations of *personal* dependence. Identity, then, was a function of a person's place within the existing social hierarchy. The emergence of capitalism, however, introduced a new relational form. Capitalism transformed feudalism's readily identifiable *personal* relations of dependence into obscure and mystified *interpersonal* relations of dependence, creating, at the same time, an impression of greater *independence*.

In the transition to capitalism, personal relations of dependence become obscured and mystified because political power passes out of the hands of individuals into the control of a distant, impersonal state apparatus. The role this apparatus assumes is one of maintaining the conditions that allow those who own the means of production to exploit those who possess only their own labor power. Within this new form of *civil society*, people's relations of dependence seemingly dissolve but are actually *intensified* as a *system* emerges, a system that *appears* to exist independent of the social relations that produced it. It is this objectification or reification of social relations, wherein "people are estranged from the means of production, from their own nature as social beings who must produce their means of subsistence in order to survive" (Burkitt, 1991, p. 9), that is responsible for the sense of alienation modern beings experience. Somewhat ironically, while capitalist social relations lead individuals to perceive themselves as if they are free of the personal ties that once bound them to their fellows, capitalism, in fact, entails greater levels of *interdependence* than any other epoch. The "objective dependency relations" of capitalism are, in fact—to borrow a phrase from Kant—the grounds of the possibility of the modern notion of self that crystallized in the eighteenth century, the theory of self that represents people as "isolated individuals":

> The further back we go in history, the more does the individual, and accordingly also the producing individual, appear as dependent and belonging to a larger whole. At first, he is still in a quite natural manner part of the family, and of the family expanded into the tribe; later he is part of a community, of one of the different forms of community which arise from the conflict and merging of tribes. It is not until the eighteenth century, in "bourgeois society" (*bürgerliche Gesell-*

*schaft*), that the various forms of the social nexus confront the individual as merely a means towards his private ends, as external necessity. But the epoch which produces this standpoint, that of the isolated individual, is precisely the epoch of the hitherto most highly developed social (according to this standpoint, general) relations. Man is a *zoon politikon* (political being) in the most literal sense: he is not just a social animal but an animal that can isolate itself *only within society* [emphasis added]. Production by an isolated individual outside society—something rare, which might occur when a civilised person already dynamically in possession of the social forces is accidentally cast into the wilderness—is just as preposterous as the development of language without individuals who live *together* and speak to one another. (Marx, 1857, in Marx, 1989)

Friedrich Nietzsche, the nineteenth-century philologist/philosopher, while not a social theorist, offers compelling evidence to support his contention that the modern notion of self is the product of sociohistorical as opposed to "natural' forces. In an aphorism entitled "The Fancy of the Contemplatives," Nietzsche draws an analogy between life and a performance, succinctly and eloquently describing how we have been seduced by "the great visual and acoustical spectacle that is life" into believing we are merely passive subjects in life's drama. The result being that "we are *neither as proud nor as happy* as we might be." The aphorism is lengthy but well worth citing in full:

What distinguishes the higher human beings from the lower is that the former see and hear immeasurably more, and see and hear thoughtfully—and precisely this distinguishes human beings from animals, and the higher animals from the lower. For anyone who grows up into the heights of humanity the world becomes ever fuller; ever more fish-hooks are cast in his direction to capture his interest; the number of things that stimulate him grows constantly, as does the number of different kinds of pleasure and displeasure: The higher human being always becomes at the same time happier and unhappier. But he can never shake off a *delusion*: He fancies that he is a *spectator* and *listener* who has been placed before the great visual and acoustic spectacle that is life; he calls his own nature *contemplative* and overlooks that he himself is really the poet who keeps creating this life. Of course, he is different from the *actor* of this drama, the so called active type; but he is even less like a mere spectator and festive guest in front the stage. As a poet, he certainly has *vis contemplativa* and the ability to look back upon his work, but at the same time also and above all *vis creativa*, which the active human being *lacks*, whatever visual appearances and the faith of all the world may say. We who think and feel at the same time are those who really continually *fashion* something that had not been there before: the whole eternally growing world of valuations, colors, accents, perspectives, scales, affirmations, and negations. This poem that we have invented is continually studied by the so-called practical human beings (our actors) who learn their roles and translate everything into flesh and actuality, into the everyday. Whatever has *value* in our world now does not have value in itself, according to its nature—nature is always value-less, but has been *given* value at some time, as a present—and it was *we* who gave and bestowed it. Only we have created the world *that concerns man*! —But precisely this knowledge we lack, and when we occasionally catch it for a fleeting moment we always forget it again immediately; we fail to recognize our best power and underestimate ourselves, the contemplatives, just a little. We are *neither as proud nor as happy* as we might be. (Nietzsche, 1974, §301, pp. 240–241)

Warren (1988) points out that, for Nietzsche, "the capacities that make subjectivity possible (intentionality, and reflexive monitoring of action) are given to the human condition, but subjectivity is not" (p. 9). "The identity of human agents," in fact, "depends not on metaphysical certainties, but on the continuity of practices, practices that are enabled by a complex of interpretations of the world and self together with a personal biography of experiences" (p. 10). Consequently, "our reflexive sense of subjectivity emerges out of practices that are enabled and constrained by experiences and interpretations" (p. 16). This is not an arbitrary process, however, for "culture and language structure and limit consciousness, and therefore provide a definite range of possibilities for self-identity" (p. 10). Individual consciousness, then, is a far from *natural* condition for human beings. It is, in fact, a state of awareness that can only be formed within a sociolinguistic nexus. "If culture," Warren argues, "provided the animal man with a social second nature, the individual—as one who possesses self-consciousness and has the capacity to act as an agent—might be thought of as a kind of 'third nature'"; in support of this contention, he asks us to "recall Nietzsche's comment that 'the human being inventing signs is at the same time the human being who becomes ever more conscious of himself. It was only as a social animal that man acquired self-consciousness—which he is still in the process of doing, more and more'" (pp. 58–59). Nietzsche's remark, made in 1882, bears an uncanny resemblance to those made by Marx some twenty-five years earlier.

Writing in the following century, the social theorist Norbert Elias (1978) offers further proof that the modern notion of the self-responsible subject is an effect of sociohistorical rather than natural forces, attributing the birth of the modern subject to fundamental social restructuring that began toward the end of Europe's Middle Ages. Elias, according to Mennell (1992, p. 37), chose "strong ground from which to fight a battle with those who see the relationship between social personality and the structure of societies as merely random." In pre-modern, medieval Europe, personal identity was "a function of predefined social roles and a traditional system of myths which provided orientation and religious sanctions to one's place in the world, while rigorously circumscribing the realm of thought and behavior" (Kellner, 1992, p. 141). Since the sense of self this feudal mode of life engendered was open neither to discussion nor reflection, it remained unproblematic for centuries.

Feudal life was disrupted, however, with the advent of the Renaissance—*circa* 1350. According to Elias (1978), during the Renaissance Europe's emergent aristocracy—a ruling elite that had begun to take shape toward the end of the Middle Ages—began forging Europe's medieval fiefdoms into centralized nation states. In order to further their own interests, the aristocracy sought to establish a new and radically different social order. But as Marx noted in 1852, while "men make their own history," they do so "not spontaneously, under conditions they have chosen for themselves; rather on terms immediately existing, given and handed down to them. The tradition of countless dead generations is an incubus to the mind of the living" (Marx, 1983b, p. 287). Europe's new ruling elite, then, had to "liberate" the populace from feudalism's oppressive traditions before a new social order could be successfully instantiated. Consequently, the aristocracy needed

to win a battle of ideas, and did so by performing two manoeuvres. One was to represent its own sectarian, class interests as universal and of democratic value, the other was to step aside from the religious ideology of the feudal epoch. Both were achieved through neo–Classicism, reviving the discourses, styles, and outward institutions of the ancient Roman imperialism. (Easthope and McGowan, 1992, p. 42)

This battle, however, was not difficult to win, for as Marx noted in 1846, "the ideas of the ruling class are in every epoch the ruling ideas. . . . The class which has the means of material production at its disposal, consequently also controls the means of mental production, so that the ideas of those who lack the means of mental production are on the whole subject to it" (Marx, 1989, p. 6). Consequently, the aristocracy was able to replace rapidly the old social order, based on the postulates of faith and tradition, with a new social order, based on the axioms of the ancient world.[4] This, Kipnis (1992, p. 377) contends, precipitated "a social transformation within which thresholds of sensitivity and refinement in the individual psyche become heightened"; the cultivation of "increasingly refined manners and habits" followed, producing a new aristocratic code of conduct. While this code functioned, initially, as "a mechanism of class distinction," it eventually restructured medieval social mores, such as, "standards of privacy, disgust, shame, and embarrassment." The "affect-reforms" of the aristocracy, Kipnis notes, were gradually

> although incompletely, disseminated downward through the social hierarchy (and finally to other nations whose lack of "civilization" might reasonably necessitate colonial etiquette lessons). These new standards of delicacy and refinement become the very substance of bourgeois subjectivity: *constraints that were originally socially generated become reproduced in individuals as habits, reflexes, as the structure of the modern psyche.* (emphasis added)

This meant one set of social mores—assumptions and presuppositions that subconsciously determine how subjects come to view their relation to the world—were replaced by another, and this, Elias (1978) contends, is the "structural change" that allows the modern self to become imaginable, a change

> reflected in self-perception, from about the Renaissance onward, in the notion of the individual "ego" in its locked case, the "self" divided by an invisible wall from what happens "outside." It is these civilizational self-controls, functioning in part automatically, that are now experienced in individual self-perception as a wall, either between "subject" and "object" or between one's own "self" and other people ("society"). (Elias, cited in Burkitt, 1991, p. 4)

The upshot, according to Burkitt (1991, p. 4), is that early-modern thinkers, such as, Descartes (1596–1650) and Locke (1632–1704), as well as modern thinkers, such as, Hume (1711–1776) and Kant (1724–1804), developed intricate metaphysical and epistemological positions to accommodate this *seemingly natural* notion of the subject. The theories they formulated served to further naturalize and reify the concept of the "self as locked inside its own thought processes and perceptions, divorced from other people and from its own emotions."

That Descartes and the Western metaphysical tradition played a central role in constructing the modern notion of the subject is most evident in the work of Martin Heidegger. While Heidegger views the "modern age, 'the age of science and technology', as one that began a few centuries ago and that is unquestioningly new," he is singular in his insistence that modernity's "true origin lies decisively if hiddenly in Greek antiquity" (Lovitt, 1977, p. xxiv–xxv). According to Lovitt, Heidegger believes that the most "fundamental Greek experience of reality was . . . one in which men were immediately responsive to whatever was presencing to them." But while "Greek man openly received and made known that which offered itself to him . . . , he tended in the face of the onrush of the revealing of Being in all that met him to seek to master it." It is "this tendency toward mastery," Heidegger argues, "that shows itself in Greek philosophy," a philosophy that "sprang from the fundamental Greek experience of reality." But because the Greek philosopher "sought to grasp and consider reality, to discover whatever might be permanent within it, so as to know what truly was," he unwittingly "distanced himself from Being, which was manifesting itself in the presencing of all particular beings." Consequently, "in his seeking, he reached out not simply to receive with openness, but also to control." Herein, Heidegger contends, "lies the real origin of the modern technological age," for Greek philosophy, "as a thinking that considered reality and therewith made it manifest in its Being, was *technē*; that is, "a skilled and thorough knowing that disclosed, . . . a mode of bringing forth into presence, a mode of revealing." In the Western tradition, then, "the metaphysical thinking born of that philosophy carried forward the expression of *technē* into modern times."

Lovitt (1977, p. xxv) notes that long after the decline of Greek civilization, the practice of metaphysics was sustained by Christian theologians, thinkers who concerned themselves with such questions as "how they might be in the right relationship with God, how they might be assured of salvation, i.e., how they might find enduring security." While such theological questions were stripped of their urgency when the Christian world view began to founder toward the end of the Middle Ages, the quest for security remained paramount to Renaissance and early-modern thinkers. Lovitt notes that, for Heidegger, "the work of Descartes, itself an expression of the shift in men's outlook that had already taken place, set forth that basis in philosophical terms." According to Heidegger, it was "in the *ego cogito (ergo) sum* of Descartes" that "man found his self-certainty *within himself,*" where "man's thinking . . . was found to contain within itself the needed sureness." From this point on, "man could *represent* reality to himself," he could "set it up over against himself, as it *appeared* to him, as an *object* of thought. This meant that "he felt assured at once of his own existence and of the existence of the reality thus conceived."

It is the epistemology of Descartes, Heidegger (1977, pp. 126–127) argues, that makes the modern conception of science—"science as research"—possible. This new mode of knowledge, "knowing, as research, calls whatever is to account with regard to the way in which and the extent to which it lets itself be put at the disposal of representation." This distinctively modern way of knowing "has disposal over anything that is when it can either calculate it in its future course in advance or verify a calculation about its past." Consequently, "nature and history become the objects of a representing that explains . . . , [but] only that which becomes object in this way *is*—is considered to be in being." Heidegger's point is that "we first arrive at science as research when the Being of whatever is, is sought in such objectiveness":

> This objectifying of whatever is, is accomplished in a setting-before, a representing, that aims at bringing each particular being before it in such a way that man who calculates can be sure, and that means be certain, of that being. We first arrive at science as research when and only when truth has been transformed into the certainty of representation. What it is to be is for the first time defined as the objectiveness of representing, and truth is first defined as the certainty of representing, in the metaphysics of Descartes.

It is with the advent of modernity that "man, once concerned to discover and decisively to behold the truly real, now finds himself certain of himself; and he takes himself, in that self-certainty, to be more and more the determining center of reality" (Lovitt, 1977, p. xxvi).

Descartes, Taylor (1987, p. 469) argues, is "the originator of the modern notion that certainty is the child of reflexive clarity, or the examination of our own ideas in abstraction from what they 'represent'." With Descartes, the traditional notion of subject—"that-which-lies-before (for the Greeks, that which looms up, e.g., an island or mountain) . . . , the reality that confronted man in the power of its presence" (Lovitt, 1977, p. xxvi)—was radically transformed. Descartes, Lovitt notes, "fixed his attention not on a reality beyond himself, but precisely on that which was present *as* and *within* his own consciousness." In this act lies the origin of the modern subject, for "at this point self-consciousness became subject *par excellence*, and everything that had the character of subject—of-that-which-lies-before—came to find the locus and manner of its being precisely in that self-consciousness," that is,

> in the unity of thinking and being that was established by Descartes in his *ego cogito* (*ergo*) *sum*, through which man was continually seeking to make himself secure. Here man became what he has been increasingly throughout our modern period. He became subject, the self-conscious shaper and guarantor of all that comes to him from beyond himself.

## AN ALTERNATIVE MODEL OF UNDERSTANDING

That the notion of a "natural" self, a conception that coalesced during the Renaissance and crystallized during the Enlightenment—the idea of a self-sufficient, rational individual, of a conscious, knowing subject that exists prior to and independent of the objects of experience—is, in fact, *untenable*, and that "*we are* first and foremost *embodied agents* in a natural and *social* world," that "our propositional knowledge of this world *is grounded in our dealings with it* and [that] there can be *no question of totally objectifying the prior grasp we have of it as agents within it*" (Baynes et al., p. 461, emphasis added) should, I hope, now be clear. But where does this leave the adult educator who must choose among competing theoretical perspectives to inform her or his practice and research?

To simply adopt the perspective of the empirical-analytic tradition because it is the preferred perspective of the establishment is to sanction a view of human beings that is highly suspect and of dubitable worth. That the "abstract individualism" of the tradition, while it grants us dominion over nature, eternally "isolates us from one another, both as objects for analysis and as subjects engaged in social intercourse" (Phelan, 1989, p. 5), is becoming abundantly clear. The problem, of course, being that "when you constitute your individual subjectivity as a self-sufficient field and a closed realm, you thereby shut yourself off from everything else and condemn yourself to the mindless solitude of the monad, buried alive and condemned to a prison cell without egress" (Jameson, 1992, p. 15). But if we cannot, as the empirical-analytic tradition suggests, "objectify" our understanding of the world, if we cannot "validate" our understanding from a disinterested and disengaged perspective, if we cannot escape our being-in-the-world, are we condemned to absolute indeterminacy and total relativism? There are those who would have us believe "that unless we can ground philosophy, knowledge, or language in a rigorous manner we cannot avoid radical skepticism" (Bernstein, 1985, p. 8). I want to suggest, however, that if we reject the empirical-analytic tradition's representational model of understanding because of its moral and spiritual consequences, we are *not* condemned to radical subjectivism. An alternative model of understanding is available to us, the very model I have used to develop my thesis that adult educators are cultural workers as opposed to technicians, and for this very reason, it is essential that they critically "evaluate received opinions," critically examine the life they are "living in the midst of the *doxae*," and come to understand their innermost selves, "the theory of whose limits and functions is among the *doxae*." This model of understanding is not without a measure of truth, but it is a measure "that, instead of being brought to bear upon the categories [of our understanding] from *without*, . . . is immanent in their own action" (Hegel, 1974, p. 147, emphasis added). The next chapter outlines how this model of understanding can be employed to make a reason-able choice among a number of competing theoretical paradigms.

# 5

# *Choosing a Research Paradigm*

> The predicament of the century is that
> so long as there is inquiry and so long
> as it is not the case that any inquiry
> whatsoever is precisely as good as any
> other, one must adopt some evaluative
> attitude toward fields of inquiry and
> their objects. Yet there is no evident
> way fully to justify casting one's eye
> over one particular field rather than
> any other, even as the realisation that
> what is seen tends to be what serves
> the institutions in power and to acquire
> the privilege of "truth" and "nature"
> through time and habit creates a felt
> need for reasons for looking where one
> does.
>
> —Wiseman, 1989, p. 1

## THE PROBLEM OF CHOICE

According to Darkenwald and Merriam (1982, p. 25): "to date, most of the significant research bearing directly on adult education has been produced by social scientists in such disciplines as psychology and sociology." The vast majority of research programs in these disciplines tend to employ a *purportedly* value-free, "positivist mode of inquiry" that is based on the empirical-analytic tradition's representational model of knowledge: a disinterested process of inquiry that proceeds from unconditioned observations of experience (uninterpreted data or

79

"facts"), via a rule-governed (hypothetico-deductive) method, to *find* the meaning (objective truth) of that which is observed. There are, however, a number of alternative modes of inquiry that are not informed by the empirical-analytic tradition's representational model of knowledge. In very general terms, these modes of inquiry can be described as "interpretive," "critical," and "postmodern."

As opposed to purportedly value-free, positivist research programs, "interpretive" modes of inquiry are *explicitly* value-laden. One of the most common interpretive research programs is that of hermeneutics: a process of inquiry that proceeds from sociohistorically conditioned observations of experience (data are "always already" interpreted), via a dialogical (the hermeneutic circle)[1] method, to recover and augment the meaning (intersubjective truth) of that which is observed. Proponents of hermeneutics contend that research is an unavoidably value-laden process and argue that the implicit technical interest of the natural sciences—the *Naturwissenschaften*[2]—is not only inappropriate for the human sciences—the *Geisteswissenschaften*—but also for the process of inquiry in general.[3] Consequently, they adopt the latter's idiographic interest in favor of the former's nomothetic interest. Since the goal of interpretive research is understanding, not prediction and control, relationships other than the strictly causal are used to explain events; therefore, hermeneutics and other interpretive research programs tend to favor qualitative, micro-analytic forms over quantitative, macro forms.

In contrast to the positivist and interpretive modes of inquiry stands a third: the "critical" mode of inquiry. While proponents of critical research programs consider the perspectives of both the *Naturwissenschaften* and the *Geisteswissenschaften* to be essential aspects of the process of inquiry, they argue that neither the former's interest of prediction and control, nor the latter's interest of understanding can deliver human beings from circumstances that are inherently dehumanizing. Advocates of the critical mode of inquiry choose as their interest *human emancipation,* employing both quantitative and qualitative forms of analysis to inform a macro theory of society as a whole—a critical social theory.

Of late, however, a fourth perspective has emerged to challenge many of the shared assumptions that inform the positivist, interpretive, and critical modes of inquiry—"postmodernism." Advocates of postmodern modes of inquiry question the very possibility of constructing "unified" research programs of any sort, since postmodernism challenges

> global, all-encompassing world views, be they political, religious or social . . . , reduces Marxism, Christianity, fascism, Stalinism, capitalism, liberal democracy, secular humanism, feminism, Islam, and modern science to the same order and dismisses them all as logocentric, transcendental totalizing meta-narratives that anticipate all questions and provide pre-determined answers. All such systems of thought rest on assumptions no more or no less certain than those of witchcraft, astrology, or primitive cults. (Rosenau, 1992, p. 6)

Despite a growing interest in interpretive, critical, and postmodern modes of inquiry, the vast majority of adult education graduate programs continue to promote positivist modes of inquiry that garner empirical-analytic knowledge.[4] The task of judging the relative merit of positivist and "postpositivist" perspectives can be a daunting one, however. How, after all, does one judge the comparative worth of modes of inquiry that proceed from fundamentally different suppositions? Kuhn (1970) contends that if there is a disagreement about the worth of a particular mode of inquiry within a community of researchers, "there is no neutral algorithm for theory-choice, no systematic decision procedure which, properly applied, must lead each individual . . . to the same decision" (p. 200). Consequently, "in the controversies that arise when new and rival paradigms are proposed . . . , there are no criteria of logical proof or any straightforward appeals to evidence that are *sufficient* to resolve the dispute" (Bernstein, 1985, p. 22). Kuhn is adamant on this point, insisting that

> like the choice between competing political institutions, that between competing paradigms proves to be a choice between incompatible modes of community life. Because it has that character, the choice cannot be determined merely by the evaluative procedures of normal science, for these depend in part upon a particular paradigm, and that paradigm is at issues. When paradigms enter, as they must, into a debate about paradigm choice, their role is necessarily circular. Each group uses its own paradigm to argue in that paradigm's defense. (p. 94)

The central contention of this chapter is that a choice among these competing research paradigms can be justified if they are viewed as logically related "moments" in a dialectical progression, such as that first described by Hegel in the *Phenomenology of Spirit* and developed in his *Science of Logic*. This should not, however, be taken as an unconditional endorsement of Hegel's philosophical system, for as Bernstein (1971, p. 8) notes: "what Hegel sometimes seems to have taken as an established truth is better understood as a heuristic principle." Marx, in fact, strongly opposed Hegel's idealist philosophy but clearly endorsed the dialectical method. Ollman (1990, p. 54), for instance, notes that Marx was convinced that "where Hegel goes wrong is in believing that the interconnections he sees in the material world are mere copies of relations existing between ideas. By turning Hegel, who was 'standing on his head', right side up, Marx corrects this error."[5]

## PROPOSING A HEURISTIC

How might adult educators choose among fundamentally different modes of inquiry if there is no common standard on which to base their judgment? This is where Hegel's notion of Dialectic proves especially fruitful, for it allows research paradigms to be judged not in terms of some *external*, meta-standard but in terms of an *internal* standard: their adequacy. For Hegel, knowledge means one thing and one thing only: Absolute Knowledge. Anything less than Absolute Truth, Hegel contends, is inadequate. On this account, any explanation that does not offer an exhaustive account of the phenomenon in question—when its *explanandum* does not exhaust the *explananda*—is inadequate: less than true. Adequacy, then, becomes the measure of worth, and a theoretical perspective that is marked by fewer inconsistencies and paradoxes, Hegel argues, is more adequate than one marred by contradictions and dilemmas. This immanent mode of critique—a critique that takes the claims of a theoretical perspective seriously and draws out their consequences—is inherent to Hegel's Dialectic. Before I move on to employ it, therefore, I need to clarify just what the notion of Dialectic entails.

While Hegel's Dialectic is often summarily described as a mechanical movement from thesis to antithesis to synthesis, such accounts fail to recognize that the Dialectic is a dynamic and organic process. It is, Bernstein (1971, p. 20) argues, a progression in which

> one "moment" of a dialectical process, when it is fully developed or understood gives rise to its own negation; it is not mechanically con-

fronted by an antithesis. The process here is more like that of a tragedy where the "fall" of the tragic hero emerges from the dynamics of the development of his own character. . . . [Subsequently,] a serious struggle takes place between the two "moments." Out of this conflict and struggle, out of this negativity, emerges a "moment" which at once negates, affirms, and transcends the "moments" involved in the struggle.

Adult educators can justifiably choose among the positivist, interpretive, critical, and postmodern modes of inquiry if they consider them as related moments in a dialectical progression: the interpretive paradigm as the antithesis of the positivist; and the critical as the synthesis of the positivist and interpretive, since it embraces aspects of each paradigm while negating others, only to transcend both. Only with the emergence of postmodernism does the notion of a dialectical progression become problematic, for while postmodernism can be construed as the antithesis of the critical paradigm, its critique calls into question the Enlightenment ideal of *progress*: "the superiority of the present over the past, the modern over the pre-modern" (Rosenau, 1992, p. 6). There are those who contest this claim, however. Langford (1992, p. 26), for instance, contends that

the Enlightenment is itself the dialectical process which continually attempts to re-create the conditions of freedom and emancipation. Rather than being a challenge to the Enlightenment, therefore, postmodernism is necessitated by it and exists not as an external critique but as a product of the ongoing dialectic that Enlightenment thought maintains with itself.

I tend to agree with Langford that postmodernism is a product, rather than a counter instance, of Hegel's Dialectic. Whether the postmodern mode of inquiry is more adequate than that of the critical mode is something that remains to be seen. To begin with, however, I want to examine the adequacy of the positivist mode of inquiry.

## POSITIVISM

While many accounts of positivism portray it as an unreflective, ingenuous world view, such accounts often fail to explain its axiomatic grip on the modern mind. Positivism, in fact, is viewed best as an amalgam or constellation of ideas that articulate together, a relational network of juxtaposed, as opposed to fully integrated, ideas that Walter Benjamin (1973) well might describe as a "forcefield" or *Kraftfeld*. It is the idea that knowledge is the internal *representation* of an outer reality, however, that provides the polarizing force for this constellation of ideas. To refute one aspect of positivism, then, does little to disturb the constellation of ideas as a whole. Keat (1981, p. 15) contends that "we can identify at least four doctrines, each of which may not unreasonably be termed 'positivist' . . . : 'scientism', 'the positivist conception of science', 'scientific politics', and 'value-freedom'." In chapter 2, I noted how these "positive" doctrines hinge upon the representational view of knowledge and articulate together to constitute a hegemonic bloc, a positivist alliance that further consolidates its power by constructing a notion of the human subject that is amenable to the forms of moral and intellectual leadership positivist forms of governance can provide.

The first positivist doctrine, *scientism*, holds that scientific knowledge is the only genuine form of knowledge, deeming all other forms—religion, metaphysics, law, politics, and ethics, for example—inferior or meaningless. The logical positivists of the Vienna Circle are, perhaps, scientism's most memorable supporters, having formulated a Verifiability Principle that proved so stringent that their own doctrine could not meet the requirements of "legitimate" knowledge.[6] Nonetheless, "in the knowledge hierarchies of postfeudal societies," according to Aronowitz (1988, pp. 8–9), "modern scientific rationality is the privileged discourse, and all others are relegated to the margins. As a result, institutions of the state as well as the economy—education systems, government bureaus, the law and criminal justice systems—emulate scientific procedures within the constraints imposed by their own traditions and exigencies."

The second positivist doctrine, *the positivist conception of science*, considers the aim of science to be that of the explanation and prediction of observable phenomena, in terms of universal, atemporal, and aspatial laws. While the truth of statements intended to express such laws is determined *solely* by their logical relationship to other nonuniversal statements that describe particular observable "data" or "facts," statements of scientific laws may contain "theoretical" terms that do not refer to observables, *but* such referents must, in principle, be observable, that is, "falsifiable." In her ovarian work, *Revolutions and Recon-*

*structions in the Philosophy of Science,* Mary Hesse (1980, p. vii) remarks of the positivist conception of science that its

> assumptions of *naïve realism,* of a *universal scientific language,* and of the *correspondence theory of truth* . . . constitute a picture of science and the world somewhat as follows: there is an external world which can in principle be exhaustively described in scientific language. The scientist, as both observer and language-user, can capture the external facts of the world in propositions that are true if they correspond to the facts and false if they do not. Science is ideally a linguistic system on which true propositions are in one-to-one relation to facts, including facts that are not directly observed because they involve hidden entities or properties, or past events or far distant events. These hidden events are described in theories, and theories can be inferred from observation, that is, the hidden explanatory mechanism of the world can be discovered from what is open to observation. Man as scientist is regarded as standing apart from the world and able to experiment and theorize about it objectively and dispassionately.

The third positivist doctrine, *scientific politics,* demands that political decisions be made according to the technical application of social scientific knowledge, as opposed to wishes, opinions, values, power, or persuasion. "Here," Keat (1981, pp. 17–18) notes, "the ideal is the use of scientific knowledge to provide rational solutions to all problems concerning the organization of society, and to free such decisions from influences of a non-scientific (and thus supposedly non-rational) kind." Since Keat finds this variant of positivism difficult to define, he refers us to a passage from Fay's (1975) *Social Theory and Political Practice,* wherein Fay contends that

> it is thought that if it were to be the case that political decisions would be made on the basis of technical application of social scientific knowledge, then the character of political argument would drastically alter. The point here is that, at least in the ideal, the disagreements that arise in engineering or medicine are not expressed in terms of personal value or wishes, nor are they debated on the basis of the power or position which the disputants have in the social order to which they belong, nor settled in terms of subtlety of exposition or rhetorical power; rather, the issues are tangible, measurable, and testable, and debates about them are conducted in such a way that it is

these objective features accessible to all which decide the matter at had. . . . If politics were to become an applied science, it is argued, its conjectural, arbitrary, emotional and personal elements would drop out, and its arguments and decisions would assume the same neutral characteristics as those of engineering. . . . In political arguments there would be, as there are in scientific arguments, reliable public standards of ascertainable truth, and therefore the possibility of a universally recognizable decisive solution to a particular problem. It is in this way that a social science would be able to eliminate the 'anarchy of opinion' which characterizes modern political thinking.

The fourth positivist doctrine, *value-freedom*, denies the very possibility of scientific politics, maintaining that it is essential to isolate the scientific realm from the political or moral realm of values. In the scientific realm, criteria that determine the validity of scientific theories, it is argued, must not refer to a moral or political position: truth or falsity must not be determined from a normative position. Furthermore, in the moral or political realm, scientific knowledge cannot be used to justify claims, for science is about what *is* the case, not what *ought* to be; consequently, people can justifiably disagree about the desirability of claims, even when such claims are established scientifically. Max Weber, one of the strongest proponents of value-freedom and keenest supporters of positive science, was also one of the first thinkers to recognize that, ultimately, scientific reason, the *sine qua non* of positivism, is *irrational*, for it serves to undermine the very possibility of that which it deigns to promote: human freedom.

Hearn (1985, pp. 74–75) notes that, "for Weber, reason or Western rationalism appears in the modern world as a technical rationality which brings to the selection of means of action methodical calculation, quantification, and predictability. *Only action which occurs consistent with this rationality is rational*" (emphasis added). Scientific reason, then,

> involves choosing the most appropriate means available for the achievement of a given goal. Purposive, planned, and calculated, rational action is predicated upon the separation of means and ends and, on another level, facts and values. Means and facts are subject to rational assessment and organization; values and ends are not. As sentiment, feeling, and custom are subordinated to deliberate calcu-

lation, rational action proceeds . . . : the fundamental characteristic of modern society. (Hearn, 1985, p. 75)

Weber recognizes, however, that while "the growth of rational action makes for an increase in freedom, . . . the spread of rational action—rationalization—restricts human freedom by enslaving people in a cold, impersonal, rationally insensitive iron cage."[7] This conundrum, according to Löwith (1982, p. 41), provides the impetus for much of Weber's work, wherein "he attempted to make intelligible this general process of the rationalisation of our whole existence precisely because the rationality which emerges from this process is something *specifically irrational and incomprehensible*" (emphasis added). Löwith notes,

> for example, [that] earning money in order to secure one's standard of living is rational and intelligible. Yet rationalised money-making for the sake of making money, 'conceived purely as an end in itself', is specifically irrational. The elementary and decisive fact is this: *every instance of radical rationalisation is inevitably fated to engender irrationality.* (emphasis added)

It is the ultimately irrational nature of the empirical-analytic tradition's scientific reason that reveals the inadequacy of the various positivist doctrines. This inadequacy is evidenced most clearly in the tradition's *explanandum* of individuals; for instance, its "beliefs in the disengaged subject, the punctual self, and described atomism" (Taylor, 1987, p. 476) leaves much about the *explananda* unexplained. As noted in the previous chapter, it is the tradition's denatured conception of human beings; of a passive, "natural" subject who "is a *spectator* and *listener* who has been placed before the great visual and acoustic spectacle that is life" (Nietzsche, 1974, pp. 240–241); of a timeless, placeless being whose meaningful experience is limited to the tangible and measurable; of a sensuous, sentient being reduced to a rule-governed, self-interested automaton—Mills' (1959) "Cheerful Robot"—that has prompted the strongest critiques of positivism.

## THE INTERPRETIVE CRITIQUE

Hans-Georg Gadamer offers one of the most forceful interpretive critiques of positivism, developing the perspective of *Philosophic Herme-*

*neutics* as the negation of not only positivism's objectifying, repressive, egocentric, domineering sovereign subject but also the representational understanding of knowledge that lies at the very core of the positivist world view. By drawing upon the work of Martin Heidegger and reintroducing the traditional German distinction between the natural sciences, the *Naturwissenschaften,* and the human sciences, the *Geisteswissenschaften,*[8] Gadamer reveals (1) that the methodology of the former is totally inappropriate for the latter, undermining scientism's aspirations of universality; (2) that prejudices are, in fact, the condition of the possibility of knowledge and not something we can ever rid ourselves of, calling into question the notion of objectivity that informs the positivist conception of science; (3) that "man always finds himself in an 'acting situation' and he is always obliged to use ethical knowledge and apply it according to the exigencies of his concrete situation" (Gadamer, 1979, p. 140), denying the possibility of a scientific politics or a value-free human science; and (4) that our disengaged representations of the world are only possible on condition that we are already "engaged in coping with our world, dealing with the things in it, at grips with them" (Taylor, 1987, p. 476), undermining the notion that knowledge, first and foremost, is comprised of our inner representations of an external reality. By focusing his attention on the "event" that comprises "Understanding," Gadamer side-steps the empirical-analytic tradition's problematic subject/object dichotomy, attributing meaning to neither the subject nor the object, but to the dialectical interplay between the two, the "happening" of Understanding.

Gadamer (1975b, pp. 446–447), in demonstrating that in the human sciences, "the fact that in the knowing involved in them the knower's own being is involved marks, certainly, the limitation of 'method'," augments the arguments of the many adult educators[9] who are convinced that

> the problem of our society is that the longing of the citizenry for orientation and normative patterns invests the expert with an exaggerated authority. Modern society expects [her or] him to provide a substitute for past moral and political orientations. Consequently, the concept of *"praxis"* which was developed in the last two centuries is an awful deformation of what practice really is. In all the debates of the last century practice was understood as application of science to

technical tasks. . . . *It degrades practical reason to technical control.* (Gadamer, 1975a, p. 312, emphasis added)

That Gadamer's *Philosophic Hermeneutics* is plagued by a number of inadequacies becomes clear, however, when certain aspects of his program are subjected to closer scrutiny. While Gadamer (1975, p. 466), for instance, is adamant that "there is undoubtedly no understanding that is free of all prejudices, however much the will of our knowledge must be directed towards escaping their thrall," he offers no clear way to distinguish "enabling prejudices"—those prejudices that lead us toward truth—from "blind prejudices"—those prejudices that distort our understanding and lead us away from truth. This also holds true in respect to claims to truth. For other than through an appeal to tradition or authority—which always remain highly questionable, at best—Gadamer offers no conclusive way to verify when the *explanandum*, our understanding of the phenomenon in question—the thing itself or *die Sache*—exhausts the *explananda*, the phenomenon in question. Bernstein (1985, pp. 154–155) argues that a *true* understanding of the thing itself must be *warranted by appropriate forms of argumentation* that are intended to show that we have properly grasped what the thing itself says," and that "it is not sufficient to give a justification that directs us to tradition," since "what is required is a form of argumentation that seeks to warrant what is valid in this tradition."

Gadamer's *Philosophic Hermeneutics*, moreover, offers no account of how power, power as a form of domination that distorts our understanding and influences our actions, impacts the modern world. As Bernstein (1985, p. 156) notes:

> Gadamer's philosophic hermeneutics is virtually silent on the complex issues concerning domination and power. But as Nietzsche, Marx, Freud, Weber, the Frankfurt thinkers, and Foucault have taught us, no intellectual orientation that seeks to illuminate concrete *praxis* in the contemporary world can be judged adequate if it fails to confront questions concerning the character, dynamics, and tactics of power and domination.

It is because of this inadequacy, because of *Philosophic Hermeneutics'* inability to critique the normative base of power relations in the modern world, that Habermas develops his critical social theory.

## THE CRITICAL PERSPECTIVE

Jürgen Habermas has developed what is arguably the most comprehensive account of a critical social theory. Habermas's (1984) *Theory of Communicative Action* can be considered the synthesis of positivism and *Philosophic Hermeneutics* because it incorporates aspects of each perspective in an attempt to transcend both. While Habermas (1972) argues *with* Gadamer against scientism's effort to equate scientific rationality with rationality in general, he argues *against* Gadamer's contention that the subordination of technical knowledge to practical knowledge is sufficient, in itself, to free human beings from the distortive and oppressive elements of tradition and authority. In accordance with the tradition of historical materialism, Habermas holds that because the very concepts we employ to investigate our understanding arise from concrete lived experiences that are *always already* shaped by asymmetrical power relations, such oppressive structures cannot be grasped or transformed by thinking about them, but only by transforming them—recall Marx's eleventh thesis on Feuerbach: "the philosophers have only *interpreted* the world in various ways; the point is to *change* it." Consequently, Habermas introduces a third form of knowledge that articulates with, rather than displaces, positivism's control-oriented, technical, empirical-analytic knowledge and Gadamer's understanding-oriented, practical, hermeneutic knowledge: a freedom-oriented, emancipatory, critical form of knowledge. While Habermas denies the emancipatory potential of both scientific and practical reason, he fully endorses the belief that liberty can be realized through the application of an universal reason, proposing his own *Universal Pragmatics* as the means to realize the Enlightenment ideal of Freedom.

Central to Habermas's *Theory of Communicative Action*, however, is the "necessary presupposition" that participants involved in communication are "unavoidably" committed to the notion that truth claims can be discursively resolved in an "ideal speech situation"; that is, in a public forum wherein the ability to speak freely and openly is not restrained by asymmetrical power relations or other coercive or distortive forces. The problem with this claim is that Habermas neglects to identify *any* conditions that would ever be sufficient to discredit it. As Bernstein (1985, p. 193) notes: "it is not helpful to say, as he [Habermas] does, that however counterfactual the ideal speech situation may be, it is anticipated and presupposed in every act of communication," for this does nothing to help us identify

> what evidence or arguments would even be relevant to refute the counterfactual claim that *despite all signs to the contrary* every speaker who engages in communicative action is committed to the presupposition of the discursive redemption of universal normative validity claims. (emphasis added)

Because Habermas is either unable or unwilling to identify the conditions that would invalidate this central presupposition, he is unable to claim scientific status for his theory, since it is not, at least in principle, falsifiable. This, of course, as Habermas is well aware, detracts from the force of his argument. But this is not the least of his problems. In demanding scientific status for his theory, Habermas fuels the very debate that spawned the positivism and scientism he and others are so critical of.

It was the fear of relativism, the fear of falling into error, that compelled early thinkers to pursue an illusory objective standard of truth. And it was the great success of the seemingly objective method of the natural sciences that precipitated the spread of scientific rationality into *all* aspects of life—scientism. While Habermas rejects scientism, contending that a practical, communicative rationality is the only form of reason appropriate for life's moral and political dimensions, he turns to scientific rationality to ground his project. In equating scientific status with truth, Habermas exhibits the same fear of falling into error that made his project necessary in the first place. In attempting to ground his *Theory of Communicative Action* in scientific rationality—a task Bauman (1992a, p. 217) describes as "a straightforward positivistic rehashing of Parsons"—Habermas subordinates communicative reason to scientific reason, not only subverting the very purpose of his project but also revealing the inadequacy of his theory.

## THE POSTMODERN PERSPECTIVE

Critical social theorists contend that postmodernism is antithetical to their emancipatory project, a project "that seeks to develop objective science, universal morality and law, and autonomous art according to their inner logic" (Habermas, 1985, p. 9), because it is inherently conservative rather than progressive. Habermas (1985, pp. 6–7), for instance, notes how the postmodernist Daniel Bell (1976), "the most brilliant of the American neoconservatives," attributes to cultural modernism all the ills "of a more or less successful capitalist modernization of the economy and society," blurring "the relationship between the welcomed process of societal modernization on the one hand, and the lamented cultural development on the other." Bell, according to Habermas, insists that

> the crises of the developed societies of the West are to be traced back to a split between culture and society. Modernist culture has come to penetrate the values of everyday life; the lifeworld is infected by modernism. Because of the forces of modernism, the principle of unlimited self-realization, the demand for authentic self-experience and the subjectivism of a hyperstimulated sensitivity have come to be dominant. This temperament unleashed hedonistic motives irreconcilable with the discipline of professional life in society, Bell says. Moreover, modernist culture is altogether incompatible with the moral basis of a purposive, rational conduct of life, In this manner, Bell places the burden of responsibility for the dissolution of the Protestant ethic (a phenomenon which had already disturbed Max Weber) on the "adversary culture." Culture in its modern form stirs up hatred against the conventions and virtues of everyday life, which has become rationalized under the pressures of economic and administrative imperatives.

But while Bell and other's of his ilk, in order to justify a legislated return to traditions that favor the West's elite, are intent upon shifting the burden of cultural decay from the productive forces of capitalism to the cultural forces of modernism's anticapitalist avant-garde, the same is not true of all postmodern modes of inquiry.

Foster (1985, pp. xi–xii), for instance, notes that "in cultural politics today, *a basic opposition* exists between a postmodernism which seeks to deconstruct modernism and resist the status quo and a postmodernism which repudiates the former to celebrate the latter: a postmodernism of *resistance* and a postmodernism of *reaction*" (emphasis added).[10] Of the two, the latter "is far better known," according to Foster, and "though not monolithic, . . . is singular in its repudiation of modernism"—a repudiation "voiced most shrilly perhaps by neoconservatives but echoed everywhere." With Habermas (1985), Foster agrees that this repudiation is unquestionably "strategic," an attack upon modernism intended to

> sever the cultural from the social, then blame the practices of the one (modernism) for the ills of the other (modernization). With cause and effect thus confounded, "adversary" culture is denounced even as the economic and political status quo is affirmed—indeed, a new "affir-mative" culture is proposed. . . . Modernism is thus reduced to a cul-tural style (e.g., "formalism" or the International style) and con-demned, or excised entirely as a cultural mistake; pre- and postmodern elements are then elided, and the humanist tradition is preserved.

Consequently, Foster agrees with Habermas that the postmodernism of reaction is little more than a thinly veiled argument for "a resurrection of lost traditions set against modernism, a master plan imposed on a heterogeneous present."[11]

## THE POSTMODERNISM OF RESISTANCE

Unlike Habermas (1985), however, Foster (1985) is not convinced that the postmodernism of resistance—which, like its reactionary counter-part, is not monolithic—is inherently regressive, recognizing that it emerges from the growing concern that *all* master plans, *all* grand schemes, whether traditional or modern, "inevitably turn into vulgar or sophisticated forms of ethnocentrism in which some privileged under-standing of rationality is falsely legitimated by claiming for it an unwarranted universality" (Bernstein, 1985, p. 19). According to Foster (1985, p. xxii),

> a postmodernism of resistance arises as a counter-practice not only to the official culture of modernism but also to the "false normativity" of a reactionary postmodernism. In opposition (but not *only* in oppo-sition), a resistant postmodernism is concerned with a critical decon-struction of tradition, not an instrumental pastiche of pop- or pseudo-historical forms, with a critique of origins, not a return to them. In short, it seeks to question rather than exploit cultural codes, to explore rather than conceal social and political affiliations.

There are, then, marked differences between postmodern modes of inquiry that seek "to question cultural codes" and "explore . . . social and political affiliations," and those that seek to "exploit cultural codes" and "conceal social and political affiliations." Unlike postmodernisms of reaction, postmodernisms of resistance do *not* value economic prosperity, political stability, and social order over all else; they also do *not* attribute prevailing social inequities to the demise of authority and tradition. Placing the ideals of freedom and equality above all else, postmodernisms of resistance refuse to relinquish the goals of the Enlightenment, even when to do so calls the very foundation of modern civilization—universal reason—into question.

While its assault upon reason leads Habermas (1985) to conclude that the postmodernism of resistance is inherently conservative—in conjunction with the postmodernism of reaction, it undermines the normative base of critical social theory, destroying the credibility of its rational arguments for change—a growing number of critical social theorists, recognizing its progressive intent and justifiable suspicion of "grand narratives" (Lyotard, 1989), are beginning to align themselves with postmodernisms of resistance that reject modernity's "totalizing" narratives but retain their emancipatory intent. Postmodernisms of resistance have proven particularly attractive to critical social theorists of a feminist and/or postcolonialist persuasion, thinkers committed to the project of modernity who found themselves constantly struggling against critical social theory's phallologo- and eurologo-centric model of rationality. Some, in order to distinguish their emergent progressive postmodernisms of resistance from regressive neoconservative postmodernisms of reaction, have taken to describing their emancipatory projects as "critical postmodernism."[12]

## CRITICAL POSTMODERNISM

With other postmodernisms of resistance, critical postmodern modes of inquiry tend to be eclectic rather than unified, idiographic rather than nomothetic, and concerned with the quotidian, rather than the eternal. But unlike other postmodernisms of resistance that reject analytic and dialectic reason, alike—due to the former's a priori principles and the latter's preordained purpose—critical postmodernisms retain dialectical logic's central notion of negation, employing it, however, to understand events in terms of their *situated meaning*, rather than the fulfillment of Hegel's World Spirit. The work of Patti Lather (1991, p. xvii) is an attempt to articulate such a critical postmodernism, an attempt to mark the development of . . . 'a critical social science' in . . . 'the postpositivist intellectual climate of our times' . . . ; to contribute to the theory and practice of liberatory education . . . ; to explore the implications of feminism, neo-Marxism and poststructuralism for developing inquiry-approaches in the human sciences that move us toward ways of knowing which interrupt relations of dominance and subordination.

Of Lather's proposed mode of research, Michael Apple (1991, p. x) writes:

Using a framework developed out of the integration of feminism, neo-marxism, and postmodernism to analyze both praxis oriented critical research and contemporary radical educational theory, Lather helps us answer a significant question. What is an empowering approach to generating knowledge? For her, all critical inquiry is fundamentally dialogic and involves a mutually educative experience. It must respond to the experiences, desires, and needs of oppressed peoples by focusing on their understandings of their situations. Its ultimate goal is to stimulate "a self-sustaining process of critical analysis and enlightened action" at the same time that it is not impositional. Coming close to Paulo Freire, Lather proposes a new, more emancipatory way of validating critical research, what she calls *catalytic validity*. Rather than researcher neutrality, she argues for a more collaborative, praxis oriented and advocacy model that acts on the desire for people to gain self-understanding and self-determination both in research and in their daily lives.

The appearance of such modes of "critical inquiry," Aronowitz and Giroux (1992, p. 187) argue, presents socially conscious, emancipatory minded educators with a whole new range of possibilities: "critical postmodernism signals the possibility for not only rethinking the issue of educational reform but also creating a pedagogical discourse that deepens the most radical impulses and social practices of democracy itself." There are those, however, who do not share Aronowitz and Giroux's unreserved enthusiasm for critical postmodernism.

Jennifer Gore (1993, pp. 34–35), for example, while an advocate of postmodernisms of resistance, is troubled by critical postmodernism because its proponents tend to favor the abstract rationale and oftentimes obtuse discourse of critical social theory. Concerned to develop pedagogical practices that engender and *embody* democratic and emancipatory ideals, rather than discuss them, she questions the emancipatory potential of a postmodern discourse grounded in a consensus-seeking critical pedagogy such as that espoused by Giroux and McLaren.[13] Of critical postmodernists Gore remarks: "their's is a discourse with theoretical and political roots in Neo-Marxism and the Critical Theory of the Frankfurt School," a discourse that "emphasizes a critique (embedded within a language of possibility) of social injustices and inequities." Their approach, she maintains, "is centered on articulating a 'pedagogical project', rather than 'pedagogical practice'; that is, a social vision for teachers' work rather than guidelines for instructional practice." Disposed to the "explicit opposition of critical pedagogy to 'dominant discourses' which prescribe practices in rather rigid and technical ways," proponents of critical postmodernism, Gore contends, tend to elide issues of practice, preferring to construct what Wexler (1987, p. 86) describes as an "abstract academic theory of practice," a practice "with no reference to any real, concrete, social movement," a "transformative pedagogy in general." In sum, critical postmodernism, for Gore, is a discourse whose "emphasis is on *the critique of oppressions and the abstract outline of possibilities* rather than on the specific actions or strategies of educators or others" (emphasis added). She concludes, therefore, that it holds little emancipatory promise.

Lather (1991, p. 16), to her credit, acknowledges that many critical "pedagogies fail to probe the degree to which 'empowerment' becomes something done 'by' liberated pedagogues 'to' or 'for' the as-yet-liberated, the 'other', the object upon which is directed the 'emancipatory' actions." While concerned to promote democratic and emancipatory practices, critical postmodernism, because it usually proceeds at the level of ideas, without "reference to any real, concrete, social movement" (Wexler, 1987, p. 86), has a tendency to fall into the trap of prescribing means that are inconsistent with its ends, seemingly forgetting that "the ends . . . 'pre-exist in the means'," that "*we become what we do, not what we wish*" (Lindeman, 1944a, p. 160, emphasis added). After engaging with students to put such a pedagogy into practice, Elizabeth Ellsworth (1989, p. 298) has this to say:

> when participants in our class attempted to put into practice prescriptions offered in the literature concerning empowerment, student voice, and dialogue, we produced results that were not only unhelp-

ful, but actually exacerbated the very conditions we were trying to work against.

Preoccupied with "dialogue" and "voice," abstract critical pedagogies, Ellsworth (1989, pp. 312–316) argues, fail to consider existing social forms wherein all voices do not "and cannot carry equal legitimacy, safety, and power." Possibly because of their origins in critical social theory, such pedagogies fail to problematize the very real issues that surround the notion of "voice." Their "conventional notions of dialogue and democracy," Ellsworth contends,

> assume rationalized, individualized subjects capable of agreeing on universalizable "fundamental moral principles" and "quality of human life" that become self-evident when subjects cease to be self-interested and particularistic about group rights. Yet social agents are not capable of being fully rational and disinterested; and they are subjects split between the conscious and unconscious and among multiple social positionings.

Because it fails to address the politics of specific educational settings in its quest to develop a general theory of practice, critical postmodernism tends to thwart its own emancipatory project. Forgetting that "democracy . . . is at bottom a mode of life founded upon the assumption that goals and methods, means and ends, must be compatible and complementary if experience is to bear creative consequences" (Lindeman, 1938a, p. 151), critical postmodernism inadvertently reproduces the material conditions that give rise to the ideas it struggles to overcome, further entrenching oppressive social forms, rather than dissolving them.

## A POSTMODERN PEDAGOGY OF ENGAGEMENT

While critical postmodernism is clearly not the antithesis of critical social theory, there are many other postmodern modes of inquiry that are truly antithetical to this position. While some are postmodernisms of reaction, a number are postmodernisms of resistance, postmodernisms that, for the purposes at hand, can be interpreted as further moments in the dialectic to realize modernity's ideals of freedom and democracy. From among these many postmodernisms of resistance, I want to focus on one, a prescription for pedagogical engagement that I think is of particular importance to adult educators. It is a program that is distinctively postmodern in its outlook, yet one that lends support to a vision of adult education articulated by Eduard Lindeman and other progressive thinkers over fifty years ago. It is a program of emancipatory and democratic practice that supports not only Lindeman's contention that adult education is the only "instrument of action" (1937, p. 76) that can establish a just social order, but also his belief that "if we genuinely want understanding . . . , we must quickly bring into existence an adult education movement which springs from the 'grass roots' of . . . life" (1945b, p. 123).

# 6

## *Toward a Postmodern Pedagogy of Engagement in Adult Education*

> Man must in some way come to his senses. He must extricate himself from this terrible involvement in both the obvious and the hidden mechanisms of totality, from consumption to repression, from advertising to manipulation through television. He must rebel against his role as a helpless cog in the gigantic and enormous machinery hurtling God knows where.
>
> —Havel, 1990, p. 11

### LIFE'S NEW AND IMPROBABLE STRUCTURES

The postmodern pedagogy of engagement I want to explore further in this chapter is one outlined and promoted by former Czechoslovakian President, Václav Havel. That Havel—whose program of resistance is adumbrated in his aptly entitled essay, *The Power of the Powerless*—is also considered a Christian Humanist should come as no surprise in our peculiarly postmodern age.[1] Most people who have heard of Václav Havel know of him either as the past president of Czechoslovakia or as the dissident playwright/poet who led his countrypeople in a courageous struggle against an oppressive, post-totalitarian, Soviet régime.[2] Few know of him as a perceptive commentator and advocate of an emancipatory project to resist the "global automatism of technological civilization" (Havel, 1978, p. 115).

99

While Havel (1978) might well reject the title of "postmodernist," being widely acknowledged for his Christian Humanist views, I believe much of what he has to say reflects the fundamental tenets of the postmodernism of resistance. He is careful, for instance, to distinguish the ideals of the Eastern Bloc's "post-totalitarian" system from the reality of the Czechoslovakian people, arguing that while Czechoslovakia's "post-totalitarian society demands conformity, uniformity, and discipline," life itself actually "moves towards plurality, diversity, independent self-constitution and self-organization"; and that while the system "contrives to force life into its most probable states," life itself "ever thrives to create new and 'improbable' structures" (p. 44). Exhibiting a typically postmodern *joie de vivre*, Havel dismisses as fiction the possibility that any totalizing system can ever meet the diverse and indeterminate needs of human life, recognizing "systemic change as something superficial, something secondary" (p. 92); consequently, he spurns abstract, technocratic, political visions. Political reality, he insists, "is not something that can be designed and introduced like a new car" (p. 71).

Havel's is a postmodernism of resistance that struggles to establish an ethical foundation for action, prescribing a program of engagement that seeks to rid Czechoslovakia of social injustice through meaningful social engagement. It is not a postmodernism of reaction, for it is "concerned with a critical deconstruction of tradition, not an instrumental pastiche of pop- or pseudo-historical forms, with a critique of origins, not a return to them" (Foster, 1985, p. xxii). Unlike neoconservative reactionaries, Havel (1990, pp. 10–11) contends that the postmodern ethos of despair stems not from an avant-garde modernism run rampant, but from a sense of loss: "the loss of metaphysical certainties, of an experience of the transcendental, of any superpersonal moral authority, and of any kind of higher horizon." With other postmodernisms of resistance, Havel's struggles to answer the question of "How . . . humans [can] be subjects of actions, historically effective and free individuals, in a world in which subjectivity is unsupported by transcendent phenomena or metaphysical essences?" (Warren, 1988, p. 7). The answer, for Havel, is through an ethically committed pedagogy of engagement such as that which contributed to the demise of the Eastern Bloc's post-totalitarian society.

## LIVING IN THE TRUTH

Havel (1978, p. 56) is keenly aware that the Eastern Bloc's post-totalitarian system strives to deny the diversity and particularity of human life, offering in its stead, the unifying ideals of a monolithic system. The system's survival, however, depends on the full cooperation of all involved. As with the "laws" of modern science, the universal "laws" of the system take on the appearance of eternal truths; consequently, only that which confirms those truths is acceptable and valued, all else is discredited, devalued, and delegitimated. What becomes clear in Havel's analysis is that the Eastern Bloc's post-totalitarian system created an ideology, a world of appearances, a mirage, a web of lies to support its idealized conception of reality. The system's continued existence, however, depends on its "Truth" remaining unchallenged, for it must be perceived as the *only* reality, not one version of reality: "as long as appearance is not confronted with reality it does not seem to be appearance."

The ultimate threat to any system, then, lies not in other idealized *conceptions* of reality, but in the *actions* of those who seek to expose systematized accounts of reality for what they really are—fabrications. This, of course, is the *sine qua non* of the postmodernism of resistance. Havel's (1978, p. 56) pedagogy of engagement seeks to establish social justice by prompting adults not only to say "the emperor is naked . . . because the emperor is in fact naked," but also to demonstrate conclusively "that living a lie is living a lie." It is a pedagogy that encourages adults, each in her or his own way, "to break through the exalted *façade* of the system and expose the real, base foundations of power"; to "peer behind the curtain"; to show "everyone that it *is* possible to live within the truth"; to reveal that "living within the lie can constitute the system only if it is universal" (since "the principle must embrace and permeate everything"); to prove that "there are no terms whatsoever on which it [the system] can coexist with living the truth, and therefore [that] everyone who steps out of line *denies it in principle and threatens it in its entirety.*"

It is because Havel (1978) denies *all* systems *any* basis for their claims to universality that I classify his pedagogy of engagement as a postmodernism of resistance. That his is a postmodernism of hope, rather than of despair, is evidenced by his rejection of the system in favor of positive and creative actions that give birth to and nurture new social "structures that are open, dynamic and small" (p. 118). Havel notes of his emancipatory project that the "ultimate phase of this process is the situation in which the official structures simply begin withering away and dying off, to be replaced by new structures that have evolved from 'below' and are put together in a fundamentally different way" (p. 108).

## A QUESTION OF INTEGRITY

While Havel's (1978, p. 54) pedagogy of engagement springs from a postmodernism of resistance that emerged in the post-totalitarian system of Eastern Europe, his analysis of its crystallization and coalescence yields some interesting questions that are pertinent not only to his fellow Czechs, but also to those of us living in the West:

> Is it not true that the far-reaching adaptability to living a lie and the effortless spread of social auto-totality have some connection with the general unwillingness of people to sacrifice some material certainties for the sake of their own spiritual and moral integrity? With their willingness to surrender higher values when faced with the trivializing temptations of modern civilization? With their vulnerability to the attractions of mass indifference? And in the end, is not the greyness and the emptiness of life in the post-totalitarian system only an inflated caricature of modern life in general? And do we [Czechoslovakians] not in fact stand . . . as a kind of warning to the West, revealing to it its own latent tendencies?

Despite such telling questions, Havel (1978, p. 85) is far from pessimistic, however, pointing out that the power of those who choose to oppose the system—*The Power of the Powerless*—lies not in directly confronting the system but in denying it in principle. Havel contends that this oppositional tactic—of making a choice to live in the truth and refusing to live in the lie—is far more effective than any form of conceptual resistance could ever be. It is a prescription for meaningful action that changes lived relations "to the point where living within the truth ceases to be a mere negation of living with the lie and becomes articulate in a particular way," to "the point at which something is born that might be called the 'independent spiritual, social and political life of society'." This "independent life," however, "is not separated from the rest of life ('dependent life') by some sharply defined line." In fact, both types of life can and do "coexist in the same people," but independent life "is marked by a relatively high degree of inner emancipation." Independent life, Havel argues,

> sails upon the vast ocean of the manipulated life like little boats, tossed by the waves but always bobbing back as visible messengers of living within the truth, articulating the suppressed aims of life. . . . In short, it is an area in which living within the truth becomes articulate and *materializes* in a visible way. (emphasis added)

The thrust of Havel's (1978, pp. 105–106) argument is that people living in the midst of oppressive systems can live an independent life if they are encouraged to turn away from the system's universalizing structures and create small, face-to-face "parallel structures," social alliances that usurp the role of the system. With courage and perseverance, the development of such alliances can contribute to the growth of movements whose primary purpose "is always . . . to have an impact on society, not to affect the power structure." Such "independent initiatives address the hidden sphere," Havel contends, demonstrating "that living within the truth is a human and social alternative" while promoting the "struggle to expand the space available for that life." In sum, "they shatter the world of 'appearances' and unmask the real nature of power."

## LIVING CAPITALISM'S LIE

Havel's analysis implies, however, that those who struggle to resist the dehumanizing forces of the West's capitalist system face a far greater challenge than their counterparts in the East. For unlike the system of the former Soviet Bloc, the system of the West has succeeded in diffusing virtually all opposition to its "progressive" modernist vision. Capitalism's representation of the truth *has had to remain* close to the lived experience of Westerners in order to retain the support of the people. The system's ideology corresponds so closely to the experience of life in the West, in fact, that the vast majority of Westerners embrace it unquestioningly as *the* truth. While the system's representation of the truth is illusory, it is not a delusion: the lived relations it re-presents are very real. It cannot, therefore, be dispelled by cries of *the emperor wears no clothes!* The product of neither a conspiracy nor a plot, capitalism's representation of the truth, Lindeman (1935a, p. 137) argues, has emerged because "we have been so busy dealing with the material problems of existence" that we have unconsciously acquiesced to modernity's overwhelmingly *rational* vision of progress. "The price we are obliged to pay for an ever-widening use of science and technology," however, "is increased conscious control over all the affairs of life" (Lindeman, 1938a, p. 149). Lindeman (1935a, p. 138) contends that in our unrelenting pursuit of progress, "we have scarcely recognized the more fundamental problem in our own personal behavior and habits": we have unwittingly submitted to "a crass, materialistic, purely external concept of life." That the people of the West are enslaved to a system that is no less oppressive than that of the East is clear to Havel (1978, p. 54), prompting his query: "in the end, is not the greyness and the emptiness of life in the post-totalitarian system only an inflated caricature of modern life in general? And do we [Czechoslovakians] not in fact stand . . . as a kind of warning to the West, revealing to it its own latent tendencies?"

## FROM INDUSTRIAL TO LATE CAPITALISM

Early in the century, Lindeman warned Westerners of the fate that awaits those who submit to modernity's systematizing impulses. Increasingly suspicious of a capitalist system that preached the ideals of freedom and equality yet failed to put them into practice, Lindeman (1944c, pp. 93–94) exhorted that

> a serious danger lies hidden in every human situation for which intellectuals have evolved elaborate rationalizations and ideas which they do not translate into experimentation. An ideal which is not practiced is . . . worse than absence of ideals. It is worse because it leads inevitably to hypocrisy, and once a human situation has become enshrouded in falsehood and misrepresentation all resolutions are postponed with the result that the situation itself becomes worse rather than better.

Lindeman (1944b, p. 155) even identified the various interests at play in the struggle for and against the system's increasing commodification of life in the West, recognizing that while democracy was expanding there was also arising within its midst, indeed at its very center, that assignment to reason which was destined in the end to destroy many of the folkways upon which democracy was created. Confronted with this dilemma, there are some who seek recovery by striving to recapture the past, by denying the rationalizations which are making life so uncertain and uncomfortable others, quite to the contrary, seek refuge in a further extension of reason, regardless of how many cherished folkways are thereby destroyed. Still a third group, to which the author belongs, seeks for a balance between these extremes, a way of resolving the two apparently contradictory laws of change and of continuity.

The struggle for and against the commodification of life continues to this day, pitting those who "seek refuge in a further extension of reason, regardless of how many cherished folkways are thereby destroyed" (modernists of a rationalist persuasion) against those "who seek recovery by striving to recapture the past, by denying the rationalizations which are making life so uncertain and uncomfortable" (antimodernist, neoconservative postmodernists of reaction) and those who seek "a balance between these extremes, a way of resolving the two apparently contradictory laws of change and of continuity" (antirationalist, antireactionary postmodernists of resistance). Fully cognizant of modernity's impersonal, inherently oppressive forces, Lindeman (1949, p. 179) warned his contemporaries that

democracy is no longer to be taken for granted. The new age, dominated by science, technology and industry, calls for a re-interpretation and a reaffirmation of our democratic way of life. We have not yet adapted ourselves to an industrial civilization. Our lives are factionalized. Our responsibilities are varied and more easily evaded. The older patterns of society from which democratic leadership emerged automatically no longer exist. Our human relations are strained; communication between professionals and laymen becomes a more hazardous undertaking. We may continue to repeat the old Eighteenth Century ideals of equality, liberty and fraternity but the world expects us to define democracy in more realistic terms. We need not forsake the old ideals but we should now undertake the task of defining democracy in the language of practice.

For Lindeman, the only feasible and realistic way of "defining democracy in the language of practice" was through adult education.

According to Lindeman: "adult education represents a groping of the people toward recognition" (1932, p. 70). It is an "educational movement" born of "discontent and unadjustment," and being "a movement is social; it starts from somewhere and moves in permeating fashion though the social mass; it originates in some form of dissatisfaction and grows as consciousness of dissatisfaction become general" (1929, p. 29). It is to be distinguished, Lindeman contends, from what often passes for adult education. His point being that "there is adult education and there is education for adults. The latter," however, which "may include everything from continuation classes in grammar, education for illiteracy, or plain vocational training to woman's club lectures and the reading of books" (1929, pp. 31–32), "is not genuine adult education. True adult education is social education" (1947, p. 55). There is no doubt in Lindeman's mind that "every social-action group should at the same time be an adult-education group, and . . . that all successful adult-education groups sooner or later become social-action groups" (1945a, p. 119).

Lindeman proposed resisting the ideas of "progress" that prevailed early in the century by engaging adults in social forms that would spawn new visions of progress, visions that would then appear as viable alternatives to those of the system. But Lindeman's is a pedagogy of engagement that, in many respects, is inherently modern. While concerned to develop an ethical, rather than an instrumental, ground for action, Lindeman assumes the existence of an underlying, universal ethic, an ethic grounded in human essence. Postmodern critiques of the notion of subjectivity that underlies this position, however, have discredited such quests as patriarchal and Eurocentric, revealing human subjectivity to be a social construct, rather than a natural, pre-existential state. Postmodernity demands an even deeper respect of difference, an even greater commitment to democracy, than a modern liberal democrat such as Lindeman could ever have envisaged. Laclau and Mouffe (1985) name this distinctively postmodern political form "radical democracy":

> "radical democracy" is . . . to be taken somehow paradoxically: it is precisely *not* "radical" in the sense of pure, true democracy; its radical character implies, on the contrary, that we can save democracy only by *taking into account its own radical impossibility*. Here we see how we have reached the opposite extreme of the traditional Marxist

[and other totalizing perspectives'] standpoint: in traditional Marx-
ism, the global solution-revolution is the condition of the effective
solution of all particular problems, while here every provisional, tem-
porarily successful solution of a particular problem entails an
acknowledgement of the global radical deadlock, impossibility, the
acknowledgement of a fundamental antagonism. (Žižek, 1992, p. 6)

## THE COMMODIFICATION OF CULTURE

Today, the capitalist system Lindeman opposed no longer exists; it has
evolved—according to Bell (1976, 1973), Foster (1989), Harvey (1989),
Jameson (1992, 1989, 1984), Lasch (1979), Lash (1990), Lash and Urry
(1987), and Tagg (1992), to name but a few—and has adopted new strategies to attain its "progressive" vision. Capitalism has entered a new
phase of "disorganized" (Lash and Urry, 1987), "post-Fordist" (Harvey,
1989), "late capitalist" (Jameson, 1992), "post-industrial" (Bell, 1973)
production, spawning, in the process, an increasingly "narcissistic"
(Lasch, 1979), "hedonistic" (Bloom, 1987) ethos, a new representation
of the truth, a new ideology, a new cultural logic—"the cultural logic
of late capitalism" (Jameson, 1992). Unprecedented technological
advances have precipitated not only the collapse of time and space but
also the proliferation of the image, effects that, in turn, have triggered
the emergence of new production techniques and marketing strategies
(Harvey, 1989; Poster, 1990). While in Lindeman's time, capitalism *had*
to offer an ideology—a representation of the truth supported by rational
justifications—that supported cultural norms in order to win the support
of Westerners, the advent of postmodernity is making this less and less
necessary.

During its "industrial" heyday, the capitalist system, while steadily
exploiting and undermining the "lifeworld" (Habermas, 1975) from
which it sprang, maintained support for its progressive vision by divert-
ing capital from material production into cultural reproduction. Unable
to explain glaring inequities in the distribution of goods during the late
fifties and early sixties, the system spawned welfare states throughout
the Western world in an attempt to add lustre to its tarnishing image.
While already subsumed by the system at this point, the cultural realm
retained a semblance of autonomy, lending credence to the system's
claim that it was still serving the interests of the lifeworld. Jhally (1989)
distinguishes this "formal" stage of subsumption from the stage that

immediately follows: the "real" subsumption of culture.[3] It is the real subsumption of culture, many contend, that marks the advent of postmodernity.

With the advent of postmodernity in the late sixties and early seventies, the capitalist system's reliance on ideology began to diminish. The modern, rational age, characterized by its "differentiated," autonomous "realms of discourse," gave way to a postmodern, nonrational age characterized by a "dedifferentiated," homogeneous "regime of signification" (Lyotard, 1989, 1988; Lash, 1990). New media technologies prompted a proliferation of images that soon far outstripped the known number of objects, images that referred not to the *real* but to other images, in a seemingly endless regress, sensory stimulants that lacked intellectual equivalents, libidinal triggers that fired *without* reason. With the advent of postmodernity, for instance, the media, according to Debord (1990, p. 19),

> proves its arguments simply by going round in circles; by coming back to the start, by repetition, by constant reaffirming in the only space left where anything can be publicly affirmed, and believed, precisely because that is the only thing to which everyone is witness. . . . there is no place left where people can discuss the realities which concern them, because they can never lastingly free themselves from the crushing presence of media discourse and of the various forces organized to relay it. Nothing remains of the relatively independent judgement of those who once made up the world of learning; of those, for example, who used to base their self-respect on their ability to verify, to come close to an impartial history of facts, or at least to believe that such a history deserved to be known.

In such a libidinal economy, rational justifications become superfluous, discourse becomes redundant, and the image rules supreme over the word. This has prompted a number of postmodernists, including Vattimo (1990), to equate the end of modernity with the end of ideology. Divested of its need to provide rational justifications for its actions, the postmodern capitalist system simply taps into the libido of Western consumers—the notion of "citizen" having long since dropped from currency—triggering desires to consume that require no rational foundation. To Westerners, postmodernity has come to mean "a shopping mall overflowing with goods whose major use is the joy of purchasing them; and existence that feels like a life-long confinement to the shopping mall" (Bauman, 1992a, p. vii). Postmodernity has produced what Tomlinson (1991, pp. 63–64) describes as a cultural void at the core of contemporary society: "what Max Weber first called 'the disenchantment of the world'—the breaking of the spell of traditional belief and practices—leaves a hole at the centre of culture which . . . cannot be filled with stories of growth and development."

In such a cultural void, how can capitalism's further erosion of culture be halted? Those who ascribe to the end of ideology thesis argue that it cannot. I tend to agree with Eagleton (1991), however, that this prognosis is premature.[4] I want to suggest that such a meaningless existence remains as a potentially grim possibility, however, if the further commodification of culture is not halted. Now, more than ever, a pedagogy of engagement is needed to create new social forms from which alternative representations of the truth can emerge. The postmodernism of resistance has revealed the intrinsically oppressive nature of traditional and rational representations of the truth. "Its job," Bauman (1992a, p. ix) contends "has been a sort of site-clearing operation":

> While renouncing what merely passes for the truth, dismantling its past, present and future putative, ossified versions, it uncovers the truth in its pristine form which modern pretensions had maimed and distorted beyond recognition. More than that: the demolition uncovers *the truth of the truth*, truth as residing in the being itself and not in the violent acts performed upon it; truth that has been belied under the domination of legislative reason. The real truth is already there before its laborious construction has started; it is re-posited in the ground on which the elaborate artifices have been erected: ostensibly to display it, in fact to hide and stifle it.

That "*the truth of the truth*" resides "in the being itself and not in the violent acts performed upon it," is evidenced in Havel's (1978) explanation of why only mutually determined, context specific *actions*, not individuated, generalized thoughts, can produce the social forms that are capable of resisting the impersonal forces of systematization. The struggle against capitalism's systematizing impulses cannot be won on the plane of ideas, at the level of discourse, alone. For discourse does little to alter the inequitable material conditions that spawn ideas of superiority and subordination. If we are to avoid the bleak fate of cultural annihilation, we must embrace a pedagogy of engagement, an adult education, that assumes the concerns expressed by Lindeman, but a pedagogy that can pursue and successfully realize distinctively postmodern conceptions of freedom, equality, and democracy: a pedagogy of practice established on the principle that "human problems cannot be 'thought through'. They must be 'lived through'"(Lindeman, 1944c, p. 94).

## ESCAPE FROM DESPAIR

Only a pedagogy of engagement, then, offers an escape from the systematizing impulses of modernity's all-encompassing scientific rationality, an escape from the dark shadows of Horkheimer and Adorno's *Dialectic of the Enlightenment*, and from Weber's terrifying vision of modernity's *bête noir*—rationalization: "bureaucratic organization . . . , a most efficient instrument of discipline and domination, a peculiarly modern form of 'unfreedom',", wherein "compliance, discipline and domination take place rationally and legally through . . . rules, regulations and procedures" (Hearn, 1985, p. 80). For those who grieve the resulting loss of certainty and objectivity, however, as for those who share Weber's (1979, p. 128) pessimistic vision of an impending, *irrational* future—"a polar night of icy darkness and hardness"—there seems little to look forward to in a postmodern age. Not everyone shares this pessimism, however. Laclau and Mouffe (1990, p. 98), for instance, declare that "there is no room for disappointment here," contending that "hopelessness in this matter is only proper to those who . . . have lived for years in a fool's paradise and then abruptly move on to invent a fool's hell for themselves." While "we have entered an age that is marked by a crisis of power, patriarchy, authority, identity, and ethics," this new "age of postmodernism," according to Giroux (1992, p. 39), "need not be one of gloom and dejection." Far from pessimistic, Laclau and Mouffe (1990, p. 98) argue that

> we are living, on the contrary, one of the most exhilarating moments of the twentieth century: a moment in which new generations, without the prejudices of the past, without theories presenting themselves as "absolute truths" of history, are constructing new emancipatory discourses, more human, diversified and democratic. The eschatological and epistemological ambitions are more modest, but the liberating aspirations are wider and deeper.

## AN AGE OF UNEASE

It would be a mistake, however, to attribute the advent of postmodernity to the forces of capitalist production, alone. Before proceeding further, therefore, I want to return—with the help of Taylor (1992)—to some important ideas that have also served as precursors to the West's prevailing cultural ethos. I began by identifying a number of adult educators who look upon our unmitigated faith in science and technology with suspicion, a faith that has led us to believe that the only way our problems can be solved is through increased capital outlays, improved and updated technologies, and increasingly refined professional and managerial techniques. While modernity's impersonal forces engineered increasing diversification and specialization and a consequent increase in social mobility, they also deeply disrupted our traditional sense of community and severed our communal ties. This disruption of community has been exacerbated by our growing reliance on professionals and technicians and a general unwillingness to seek communal solutions to our problems. In fact, "the failure of contemporary reason and rationality is that the transformation of the sacred into notions of modern science and technology has stripped away a prerequisite for community. Everything seems scattered and rootless" (Popkewitz, 1992, p. 135). This is the denaturing process Weber (1979) describes as the "disenchantment of the world." The situation is now such that we are experiencing a "cultural redefinition (some call it a breakdown) and loss of collective traditions and future" (Popkewitz, 1992, p. 135). While Taylor and others (cf. Berman, 1982) view this crisis to be a further consequence of modernity, many, as we have seen, attribute it to the emergence of distinctively "post" modern forces.

## THE MODERN INDIVIDUAL

Taylor (1992, pp. 2–12) suggests the cultural disintegration that Popkewitz alludes to can be attributed to three factors: (1) the emergence of individualism, (2) the deification of scientific reason, and (3) a loss of personal freedom. For many, individualism is the greatest achievement of modernity. The modern world is one in which "people have a right to choose for themselves their own pattern of life, to decide in conscience what convictions to espouse, to determine the shape of their lives in a whole host of ways that their ancestors couldn't control." Individualism means that "people are no longer sacrificed to the demands of supposedly sacred orders that transcend them." But such freedom is only possible when the ties to "older moral horizons," rigid social hierarchies that emulated the "great chain of Being"—the single over-arching cosmological order "in which humans figured in their proper place along with angels, heavenly bodies, and our fellow earthly creatures"—are severed. While this break with the past freed individuals from the restrictive conventions and traditions that locked them "into a given place, a role and station that was properly theirs and from which it was almost unthinkable to deviate," it also severed their ties to the structures that had long given meaning to life: "the rituals and norms [that] had more than merely instrumental significance." Consequently, "the individual lost something important along with the larger social and cosmic horizons of action." This loss was of life's "heroic dimension," of its sense of "higher purpose," a loss that was compounded as "people lost their broader vision because they focussed on their individual lives." This is the "dark side" of individualism, "a centring on the self . . . which both flattens and narrows our lives, makes them poorer in meaning, and less concerned with others or society." The seeds of "narcissism" and "hedonism" are clearly evident here.

## INSTRUMENTAL REASON

The second factor that contributes to the disenchantment of the world, according to Taylor (1992, pp. 4–8), is the ascendancy of scientific or instrumental reason: "the kind of rationality we draw on when we calculate the most economical application of means to a given end. Maximum efficiency, the best cost-output ratio, is its measure of success." Because we no longer live in a world that is "grounded in the order of things or the will of God," a world that has no preordained goals, all things seem to be "up for grabs" and amenable to being "redesigned with their consequences for the happiness and well-being of individuals as our goal." Consequently, "the yardstick that henceforth applies is that of instrumental reason" and the world and its creatures become "open to being treated as raw materials or instruments for our projects." Accompanying the liberating impulse of instrumental reason, however, is a certain fear, a fear "that things that ought to be determined by other criteria will be decided in terms of efficiency or 'cost-benefit' analysis, that the independent ends that ought to be guiding our lives will be eclipsed by the demand to maximize output." Taylor suggests many things substantiate this worry; for instance, "the ways the demands of economic growth are used to justify very unequal distributions of wealth and income" and "the way these same demands make us insensitive to the needs of the environment, even to the point of potential disaster, or the way in which "much of our social planning, in crucial areas like risk assessment, is dominated by forms of cost-benefit analysis that involve grotesque calculations, putting dollar assessments on human lives."

The sovereignty of instrumental reason, Taylor (1992, pp. 6–8) argues, is particularly evident in our growing reliance on technology, an unquestioned faith that leads us to believe that we should pursue technological solutions to all our problems, even in the realm of health care. This technological approach "has often side-lined the kind of care that involves treating the patient as a whole person with a life story, and not as the locus of a technical problem." This is particularly evident in the way that "society and the medical establishment frequently undervalue the contribution of nurses who provide this humanly sensitive caring, as against that of specialists with high-tech knowledge." The primacy of instrumental reason and the dominance of technology, along with individualism's preoccupation with the self, have contributed to "the narrowing and flattening of our lives," to the "loss of resonance, depth, or richness in our human surroundings." Our predicament is now such that, more and more, "powerful mechanisms of social life press us in this direction"; consequently, "a manager in spite of her own orientation may be forced by the conditions of the market to adopt a maximizing strategy she feels is destructive," or "a bureaucrat, in spite of his personal insight, may be forced by the rules under which he operates to make a decision he knows to be against humanity and good sense." It is this insidious impulse to "rationalize" all aspects of life that steers us, ineluctably, toward Weber's "iron cage." What some view to be a peculiarly "post" modern tension, between the rational and the nonrational, is clearly evident here.

## THE LOSS OF PERSONAL FREEDOM

The final result is, according to Taylor (1992, p. 10), that "the institutions and structures of industrial-technological society severely restrict our choices"—our personal freedom—forcing "societies as well as individuals to give a weight to instrumental reason that in serious moral deliberation would never do, and which may even be highly destructive." The forces that determine the direction of societies structured around instrumental reason impose "a great loss of freedom, on both individuals and the group," making it increasingly difficult to sustain an individual life-style that runs "against the grain." Such societies, moreover, comprised as they are of individuals "enclosed in their own hearts," are not conducive to participation and active self-government, making them particularly susceptible to what Alexis de Tocqueville called "soft" despotism. While this "will not be a tyranny of terror and oppression as in the old days," since "the government will be mild and paternalistic" and "may even keep democratic forms, with periodic elections," it will, nonetheless, be despotic because "everything will be run by an 'immense tutelary power', over which people will have little control." Consequently, "the only defence against this . . . is a vigorous political culture in which participation is valued, at several levels of government and in voluntary associations as well." The problem, however, is that "the atomism of the self-absorbed individual mitigates against this," and "once participation declines, once the lateral associations that were its vehicles wither away, the individual citizen is left alone in the face of the vast bureaucratic state and feels, correctly, powerless." Not surprisingly, this estrangement from the public sphere "demotivates the citizen even further," further contributing to "the vicious cycle of soft despotism." Once, however, we become caught in this spiral of despair,

> what we are in danger of losing is political control over our destiny, something we could exercise in common as citizens. This is what Tocqueville called "political liberty." What is threatened here is our dignity as citizens. The impersonal mechanisms mentioned above may reduce our degrees of freedom as a society, but the loss of political liberty would mean that even the choices left would no longer be made by ourselves as citizens, but by irresponsible tutelary power.

Thus, three features of modernity—the first, according to Taylor (1992, p. 10), being "what we might call a loss of meaning, the fading of moral horizons. The second concerns the eclipse of ends, in the face of rampant instrumental reason. And the third is about a loss of freedom"—have contributed to the establishment of social forms that make it exceedingly difficult for socially conscious, emancipatory minded adult educators to engage learners in democratically oriented forms of education that seek to create just and equitable societies. That scientific rationality has usurped the role of practical wisdom is clear not only to Lindeman (1961) but also to Gadamer (1975b, p. 312), who argues that "the problem of our society is that the longing of the citizenry for orientation and normative patterns invests the expert with an exaggerated authority. Modern society expects [her or] him to provide a substitute for past moral and political orientations." This "peculiar falsehood of modern consciousness," Gadamer contends, has subjugated "the noblest task of the citizen—decision-making according to one's own responsibility—instead of conceding that task to the expert."

It is not, however, simply that people have relinquished their right to participate in the decision-making processes that affect their lives, it is that they have lost the *desire* to do so, due, to a large extent, to the impersonal forces, first, of modernity and subsequently of postmodernity. Since modern, scientific and technicized adult education practices have played an important role in this denaturing process, it is imperative that adult educators recognize the moral and political consequences of their practice and research and that they actively seek to re-involve adults in the decision-making processes that are an integral aspect of their lives. This demands a pedagogy of engagement that must do two things: (1) it must proceed in a manner that alerts adults to the impersonal forces of modernity that are denying them the right to make responsible decisions and stripping them of their dignity, and (2) it must *engage* adults in democratic practices as well as provide them with the communicative and critical competencies to resist the further sytematization of culture. Such a pedagogy of engagement is perhaps the only means of establishing just and equitable communities of citizens that can resist the systematic annihilation of culture.

## IMPLICATIONS FOR PRACTICE

What does all this mean for the adult educator who is struggling to find an ethical basis for her or his research and practice? It means, first of all, that the security and certainty of scientific rationality has to be relinquished if the *intent* of the Enlightenment's emancipatory project is ever to be realized. Scientific rationality, once thought to be the panacea for all that ailed humanity, has proven to be an anti-democratic, totalizing force, with regard neither for nature nor human beings. McLaren (1993, p. 121), for instance, writes that

> Enlightenment reason mocks us as we allow it to linger in our educational thinking and policies; for some of the most painful lessons of modernity have been that a teleological and totalizing view of scientific progress is antipathetic to liberation; that capitalism has posited an irrecuperable disjunction between ethics and economics and that, paradoxically, modernity has produced an intractable thralldom to the very logic of domination which it has set out to contest and in so doing has reproduced part of the repression to which it has so disdainfully pointed.

Secondly, it means coming to terms with the fact that adult education is and always has been, in Foucault's (1972) sense, a "discursive formation." As a practice, adult education existed long before it was named and operationalized in the quest for professionalization, and the struggle to define the field's boundaries, to include and legitimate certain practices while excluding and delegitimating "others," continues to this day, despite the establishment's efforts to construct a "central" discipline. Thirdly, it means acknowledging that adult education is a sociohistorical and political practice, not a range of techniques and instructional methodologies devoid of human interest. Fourthly, it means recognizing that in this "post" modern period, "all that modernity has set aside, including emotions, feelings, intuition, reflection, speculation, personal experience, custom, violence, metaphysics, tradition, cosmology, magic, myth, religious sentiment, and mystical experience . . . takes on a new meaning" (Rosenau, 1992, p. 6). Fifthly, it means realizing that the purported nihilism of the postmodernism of resistance "does not signify its rejection of ethics, politics, and power, only its refusal to accept the givens of public and private morality and the judgments arising from them" (Giroux, 1991, p. 187). Ultimately, it means coming to terms with post-ideological or post-hegemonic forms of adult education practice, with adult education as a pedagogy of engagement.[5]

Since many of the issues that a pedagogy of engagement must address are identified by Hall (1992, p. 278) in a discussion related to the postmodern practice of cultural studies, I have taken the liberty of

substituting *a pedagogy of engagement* for the term *cultural studies* in
the extract from Hall's essay that appears below:

> Now, does it follow that *a pedagogy of engagement* is not a policed
> disciplinary area? That it is whatever people do, if they choose to call
> or locate themselves within the project and practice of *a pedagogy of
> engagement*? I am not happy with that formulation either. Although
> *a pedagogy of engagement* as a project is open-ended, it can't be sim-
> ply pluralist in that way. Yes, it refuses to be a master discourse or a
> meta-discourse of any kind. Yes, it is a project that is always open to
> that which it doesn't yet know, to that which it can't yet name. But it
> does have some will to connect; it does have some stake in the
> choices it makes. It does matter whether *a pedagogy of engagement*
> is this or that. It can't be just any old thing which chooses to march
> under a particular banner. It is a serious enterprise, or project, and that
> is inscribed in what is sometimes called the "political" aspect of *a
> pedagogy of engagement*. Not that there's one politics already
> inscribed in it. But there is something *at stake* in *a pedagogy of
> engagement*, in a way that I think, and hope, is not exactly true of
> many other very important intellectual and critical practices. Here
> one registers the tension between a refusal to close the field, to police
> it and, at the same time, a determination to stake out some positions
> within it and argue for them. That is the tension—the dialogic
> approach to theory . . . [that this text argues for in proposing a peda-
> gogy of engagement]. I don't believe knowledge is closed, but I do
> believe that politics is impossible without what I have called "the
> arbitrary closure" without what Homi Bhabha called social agency as
> an arbitrary closure. That is to say, I don't understand a practice
> which aims to make a difference in the world, which doesn't have
> some points of difference or distinction which it has to stake out,
> which really matter. It is a question of positionalities. Now, it is true
> that those positionalities are never final, they're never absolute. They
> can't be translated intact from one conjuncture to another; they can-
> not be depended on to remain in the same place.

The challenge, then, to those who wish to pursue a pedagogy of
engagement, is threefold: it is (1) to embrace "the tension between a
refusal to close the field, to police it and, at the same time, a determina-
tion to stake out some positions within it and argue for them"; (2) to
recognize that while practice or "knowledge is not closed," there are
times when theoretical or "arbitrary closure" must be brought to defend

"points of difference or distinction," to "stake out" issues that demand political resolutions; and (3) to remember, however, that such solutions are always "a question of positionalities," solutions that "are never final, . . . never absolute," solutions that "can't be translated intact from one conjuncture to another," solutions that "cannot be depended on to remain in the same place." It is, then, to agree with Lindeman (1944c, p. 94) not only that "life is a matter of compromises," but also that "there are two types of compromise, one of which leads upward and onward to improvement and the other downward towards deterioration." It is to recognize that "the former variety of compromise is always attached to practicable experiment and the latter to legal or logical abstractions." It is to realize that "when we plan for the improvement of education . . . we are speaking of education for the purposes of action . . . , of the human issues which trouble us," and that "human problems cannot be 'thought through'. They must be 'lived through'."

As Butler (1987, p. 145) notes, this is to place great emphasis on "meaning as a contested event, a terrain of struggle in which individuals take up often conflicting subject positions in relation to signifying practices," and to insist that "meaning consists of more than signs operating and being operated in a context. It is to realize that "there is a struggle over signifying practices," and that "this struggle is eminently *political* and must include the relationship among discourse, power, and difference," as well as "the contradictions involved in subject formation." This is to acknowledge that "the subject is a consequence of certain rule-governed discourses that govern the intelligible invocation of identity. The subject is not *determined* by the rules through which it is generated because signification is *not a founding act, but rather a regulated process of repetition* that both conceals itself and enforces its rules precisely through the production of substantializing effect." According to Butler, it is only through a process of interpersonal engagement, then, that adult educators can come to realize that

> there is no self that is prior to the convergence or who maintains "integrity" prior to its entrance into this conflicted cultural field. There is only a taking up of the tools where they lie, where the very "taking up" is enabled by the tool lying there. . . . We construct our future selves, our identities, through the availability and character of signs of possible futures. The parameters of the human subject vary according of the discursive practices, economies of signs, and subjectivities

(experiences) engaged by individuals and groups at any historical moment. [In fine,] we must abandon the . . . idea that we posses as social agents a timeless essence or a consciousness that places us beyond historical and political practices. Rather, we should understand our working identities as an effect of such practices . . . : our identities as subjects are . . . constitutive of the literacies we have at our disposal through which we make sense of our day-to-day politics of living.

The political problems that arise from abandoning the belief that "we possess as social agents a timeless essence or a consciousness that places us beyond historical and political practices" may, perhaps, be resolvable through strategies such as that suggested by Laclau and Mouffe (1985)—see Žižek's (1992) account of "radical democracy" above. Ultimately, however, solutions, if they are to be authentic, must arise from concrete practices, not abstract theories—for "human problems cannot be 'thought through'. They must be 'lived through'" (Lindeman, 1944c, p. 94). What this means is that adult educators must relinquish their roles as technicians and embrace their responsibility as cultural workers. To embrace a pedagogy of engagement is to acknowledge that discourse "is bounded by the historical, cultural, and political conditions and the epistemological resources available to articulate its meaning. . . . People do not possess power but produce it and are produced by it in their relational constitution through discourse" (Butler, 1987, p. 145).

As self-confessed cultural workers, it is essential that adult educators critically "evaluate received opinions," critically examine the life they are "living in the midst of the *doxae*," and come to understand their innermost selves, "the theory of whose limits and functions is among the *doxae*." Only through *engaging with others* in a process of *mutual* self-examination will adult educators be able to "grasp and represent the commonalities of subordinate groups' experiences as historically changing and changeable . . . , and to do so without reducing their differences to an essential or universal standpoint" (Roman, 1993, p. 175). Only through a pedagogy of engagement will adult educators be able to recognize that "discourses are not single-minded positivities but are invariably mutable, contingent, and partial," that "authority is always provisional as distinct from transcendental," and that while "discourses may in fact *possess* the power of truth, . . . in reality they are historically contingent rather than inscribed by natural law; they emerge out of social conventions" (Butler, 1987, p. 145).

# Postscript

## Living through the Question
## of Adult Education

> To theorise, one leaves home.
> —Clifford, 1989, p. 177

There are some telling silences in this inquiry. I had planned, based on the recommendation of colleagues, to address them in a final chapter. Grounded in my own lived experience, its focus was to be practical, rather than theoretical, aimed at identifying problems associated with putting a pedagogy of engagement into practice. Problems, for instance, associated with choosing readings, scheduling assignments, determining workloads, categorizing "learners," recognizing differences—of gender, age, race, class, sexual preference, religion, etc.—distributing power, facilitating free speech, the list goes on. These are *lived* problems that educators face every day. I find myself struggling, however, to think and write about these practical concerns in a way that does not subjugate them to the abstract and decontextualized ideas that have come to dominate lived experience, in a way that does not promote "the basic sophistry whereby the philosophico-epistemological notion of space is fetishized and the mental realm comes to envelop the social and physical ones" (Lefebvre, 1991, p. 5).

My struggle with this problem has led me to realize that I have always assumed that a correlation existed between the world as experienced and the world as thought, and in reflecting upon the study I have just completed, I now recognize that

> what is happening [t]here is that a powerful ideological tendency, one much attached to its own would-be scientific credentials, is express-

121

ing, in an admirably unconscious manner, those dominant ideas which are perforce the ideas of the dominant class. To some degree, perhaps, these ideas are deformed or diverted in the process, but the net result is that a particular "theoretical space" produces a mental space which is apparently, but only apparently, extra-ideological. In an inevitably circular manner, this mental space then becomes the locus of a "theoretical practice" which is separated from social practice and which sets itself up as the axis, pivot or central reference point of Knowledge. (Lefebvre, 1991, p. 6)

Premised on the existence of a "mental space which is apparently, but only apparently, [I now realize] extra-ideological," the study takes the form of a "theoretical practice" that "creates an abyss between the mental sphere on one side and the physical and social spheres on the other," of a theoretical practice that proceeds from "the quasi-logical presupposition of an identity between mental space (the space of philosophers and epistemologists) and real space." Consequently, it unwittingly subjugates the concrete, lived experience of the physical and social realms to the analytic thought and abstract discourse of the mental realm. For on this view, "no matter how relevant, the problem of knowledge and the 'theory of knowledge' have been abandoned in favour of a reductionist return to the absolute—or supposedly absolute—knowledge" (Lefebvre, 1991, p. 6).

While this is not the position I wished to support, nor the one I consciously hold, the study is evidence of my *unconscious* belief that thoughts and discourse *about* practice can be translated into truths *of* practice, that the truths of the physical and social realms can be accessed through the mental realm. Before I tackle the problems associated with putting a pedagogy of engagement into practice, then, I need to spend some time living, rather than thinking, through these problems, for I remain convinced that

the body does not fall under the sway of analytic thought and its separation of the cyclical from the linear. The unity which that reflection is at such pains to decode finds refuge in the cryptic opacity which is the great secret of the body. For the body indeed unites cyclical and linear, combining the cycles of time, need and desire with the linearities of gesture, perambulation, prehension and the manipulation of things—the handling of both material and abstract tools. The body subsists precisely at the level of the reciprocal movement between these two realms; their difference—which is lived, not thought—is its habitat. Is it not the body, in fact, since it preserves difference within repetition, that is also responsible for the emergence of the new from the repetitive? Analytic thought, by contrast, because it evacuates difference, is unable to grasp how repetition is able to secrete innovation. Such thought, such conceptualizing knowledge (*connaissance*), cannot acknowledge that it underwrites the body's trials and tribulations. Yet, once it has ensconced itself in the gap between lived experience and established knowledge (*savoir*), the work it does there is in the service of death. An empty body, a body conceived of as a sieve, or as a bundle of organs analogous to a bundle of things, a body "dismembered" or treated as members unrelated to one another, a body without organs—all such supposedly pathological symptomatology stems in reality from the ravages of representation and discourse, which are only exacerbated by modern society, with its ideologies and contradictions. (Lefebvre, 1991, pp. 203–204)

# *Notes*

## PREFACE

1. A product of the "gap" that exists between the rational and irrational elements of the modern self, the phenomenon of disavowal is readily identifiable in Mannoni's often quoted "I know very well, but all the same. . . ." See Metz (1982, pp. 69–76) for an insightful introduction to Mannoni's dictum.

## CHAPTER 1. ENGAGING THE QUESTION OF ADULT EDUCATION

1. Being versed in literary theory and philosophy rather than psychology and quantitative analysis, I remembered being struck by the irony of this statement. The modern practice of adult education had reduced the realm of "practice," long recognized in the Western philosophical tradition to be a sphere so vast and indeterminable that outcomes could never be predicted in accordance with a set of universal "rules"— Aristotle, for instance, holds that "the rule of the undetermined is itself undetermined" (*Nicomachean Ethics*, 1137b, 29–3)—to a mechanistic realm of empirical facts ruled by common sense, to a sphere of life so shallow and determinable that all and every outcome can be extrapolated, in principle, from nothing more than a detailed observation of the data. Far from "practical," it seemed to me that the modern practice of adult education is an irrefutably positivist enterprise, a distinctively technical endeavor concerned solely with the discovery and application of "universal" laws of experience in accordance with the tenets of empirical science.

## CHAPTER 2. THE FEAR OF FALLING INTO ERROR

1. The term *idea* is used in the very general sense of belief and is used interchangeably with the term *concept* to refer to what is generally agreed to be our intramental understanding of an extramental reality.

2. See E. Halévy (1986) and P. Freire (1974).

3. Others include Bright (1989); Briton and Plumb (1993a, 1993b, 1992a, 1992b); Brookfield (1990, 1989, 1985); Cervero and Wilson (1994); Collard and Law

(1988); Collins (1987, 1988); Cruikshank (1991); Cunningham (1989; 1992); Fieldhouse (1981); Finger (1988); Greene (1990); Hart (1990a, 1990b, 1985); Heaney and Horton (1990); Hellyer and Schied (1984); Law (1992); Mezirow (1985, 1990); Plumb (1989); Rockhill, Carlson, and Davenport (1982); Rubenson (1982); Schied (1993, 1992); Taylor, Rockhill, and Fieldhouse (1985); Thompson (1980); Thorpe, Edwards, and Hanson (1993); Usher (1989); Usher and Edwards (1994); Welton (1990, 1991, 1995); Westwood and Thomas (1991); and Zacharakis-Jutz (1992, 1989).

4. See Briton and Plumb (1993a) for a sketch of this professionalization process.

5. Logical positivism, which dominated scientific thought during this period held that "for a sentence to have 'cognitive', 'factual', 'descriptive', or 'literal' meaning . . . , it must express a statement that could, at least in principle, be shown to be true or false, or to some degree probable, by reference to empirical observations" (Ashby, 1967, p. 240).

6. A variation of this argument can be found in Briton and Plumb (1993b).

7. The parochial concerns of early adult educators, Wilson (1991) argues, is evident from the nature of the submissions to the 1934 *Handbook of Adult Education in the United States*—D. Rowden (ed.). New York: American Association for Adult Education.

8. According to Habermas (1987, p. 2):

"modernization" was introduced as a technical term only in the 1950s. It . . . refers to a bundle of processes that are cumulative and mutually reinforcing: to the formation of capital and the mobilization of resources; to the development of the forces of production and the increase in the productivity of labor; to the establishment of centralized political power and the formation of national identities; to the proliferation of rights of political participation, of urban forms of life, and of formal schooling; to the secularization of values and norms; and so on."

9. See Wilson's (1992) historical analysis of the field's preoccupation with empirical-analytic knowledge.

10. Marcuse was one of several expatriate Germans who continued the critical social theory of the *Institut fur Sozialforschung* (the Institute for Social Research) in the United States during and after World War II. Other members of the so-called Frankfurt School were Grunberg, Horkheimer, Lowenthal, Pollock, Fromm, Grossman, Adorno, Kirchheimer, Neumann, Korsch, and Benjamin. For a succinct account of the origins of critical social theory, see Kellner (1990).

11. The outline for this work was, in fact, constructed in this manner.

12. Mead (1981) was one of the first non-Continental proponents of the view that our notions of the "mind" and "self" are formed within the communicative activity of the social group. Hegel, of course, had suggested as much in the *Phenomenology of Spirit*, in 1807, and Nietzsche, in *The Will to Power*, in 1901. For other theories of self-formation that challenge that of the rational, autonomous subject see Lévi-Strauss'

(1975), Althusser's (1971), and Lacan's (1977a, 1977b) structuralist theories of self-formation, and Foucault's (1970, 1977, 1982) and Baudrillard's (1983) poststructuralist accounts of self-formation.

13. For a discussion of the role English grammar schools played in the shaping of modern subjectivity, see Corrigan (1991).

## CHAPTER 3. FACING THE DILEMMA

1. See, for instance, Anyon (1980); Apple (1979, 1986); Barton, Meighan, and Walker (1980); Bourdieu and Passeron (1977); Bowles and Gintis (1977); Carr and Kemmis (1986); Giroux (1981); Whitty and Young (1977); and Willis (1983).

2. Wilson's (1991, p. 1) analysis of the adult education handbooks published between 1934 and 1989 reveals that (1) "empirical-analytic knowledge is the dominant form of knowledge in adult education," (2) "university researchers in the field of adult education have relied on empirical-analytic knowledge to develop the knowledge base of adult education in order to control the development of the field as a profession," and (3) "this professionalization process depends on using empirical-analytic knowledge to standardize professional practice in order to develop a market share in a service economy, to systematize both the practice and training of practitioners, and to use science as a solution to social problems."

3. This offensive against the scientific establishment's seamless construal of scientific practice, a construal supported by evidence culled from a very cautiously reconstructed and "selective tradition" (Williams, 1961), is not unlike the attack historically minded "radical revisionists" have launched upon the adult education establishment's seamless construal of adult education practice. Wilson (1991, p. 7) notes that the establishment's equally selective account of the field's development, an account that imagines "the adult education 'movement' heading inexorably toward professional fruition," is strenuously contested by historically minded adult educators, educators such as Collins (1992, 1991), Cunningham (1989), Hellyer and Schied (1984), Rockhill (1984), Welton (1991, 1987a, 1987b), and Zacharakis-Jutz (1992, 1989). Schied (1993, p. xii), for instance, argues that

> the real issue is that dominant adult education historiography has given us a censored version of our own past. It has reduced to marginal status those groups and individuals involved in social change activities. This marginality denies the central role groups dedicated to social change have played in adult education. By denying educators the possibility of knowing an alternative historical conception of the field, mainstream adult education history denies the very existence and experiences of people who have challenged the dominant society.

4. Those who doubt that epistemologists do not view their task to entail much more than the verification of claims to truth need look no further than Karl Popper's *The Open Society and Its Enemies.* In this diatribe against Hegel and Marx, Popper, epistemology's theorist *par excellence*, attacks the Hegelian/Marxist tradition, not

because of its epistemology—a sphere in which, some contend, he is eminently qualified to make judgments—but because he opposes the moral and political implications of that tradition—a sphere in which, it would seem, he is eminently unqualified to make judgments: see Popper (1988).

5. I say with some reservations because Hebdige and others reject Althusser's contention that the forces of ideology cannot be resisted. Hebdige holds that while ideological forces play an important role in shaping subjectivity, they can be opposed.

6. Note that while Hebdige recognizes that ideology places certain things "beyond question," representing them as "givens," he insists that the world "can, of course, be altered."

7. In the introduction to *The Phenomenology of Spirit*, Hegel dismisses the representational understanding of knowledge, a model that proceeds from how things *appear* to be, as ingenuous. If knowledge is construed, as this model implies, as an "instrument" that grasps the Truth or as a "medium" through which the Truth passes, removing the distortive effect either medium imposes leaves one with no better understanding of the Truth than when one began.

8. A *camera obscura* was a medieval device popularized in the nineteenth century, a darkened box wherein the image of an object, received through a small aperture, was projected, *upside-down*, on a rear surface for viewing or tracing. The problem of inversion was eventually rectified with the help of a lens. See Crary (1990) for an extended discussion of the *camera obscura*.

## CHAPTER 4. ENLIGHTENMENT AND MODERNITY

1. Wiseman (1989, p. 3), for example, contends that "modernist painters are said to have seen through layers of convention governing the illusionistic representation of the look of the world to the very fundaments of form; modernist architects to have seen through layers of decoration, seen through painted faces to sculpted forms, but to forms sculpted by function alone."

2. A quote from Horace, *Sapere Aude!* translates as Dare to Know! the motto of the Society of the Friends of Truth, a German Enlightenment movement.

3. Marx (1818–1883), in terms of feudal and capitalist modes of production; Spencer (1822–1903), in terms of military and industrial societies; Weber (1864–1920), in terms of traditionalism and rationalization; Maine (1822–1988), in terms of status and contract; Tönnies (1855–1936), in terms of *Gemeinschaft* and *Gesellschaft;* Durkheim (1858–1917), in terms of mechanical and organic solidarity; and Simmel (1858–1918), in terms of non-monetarized and monetarized economies (Sayer 1991, Hoogvelt 1982).

4. It is under the rubric of *"transcendental social action"* that Dear and Wolch (1991, pp. 8–9) describe social transformations of this nature, that is, change that

"occurs through the autonomous actions of classes and groups within the economic, political, and social spheres."

## CHAPTER 5. CHOOSING A RESEARCH PARADIGM

1. Geertz (1979, p. 239) describes succinctly the methodology of the hermeneutic circle: "a continuous dialectical tacking between the most local of local detail and the most global of global structures in such a way as to bring both into view simultaneously."

2. "In the Anglo-American tradition, intellectual disciplines fall into the trichotomy of the natural sciences, social sciences, and humanities, but on the Continent they are categorized according to the dichotomy between the *Naturwissenschaften* and the *Geisteswissenschaften* (the expression that was introduced into German as a translation for what Mill called the 'moral sciences'). In the main tradition of Anglo-American thought—at least until recently—the overwhelming bias has been to think of the social sciences as *natural sciences* concerning individuals in their social relations. The assumption has been that the social sciences differ in the degree and not in kind from the natural sciences and that ideally the methods and standards appropriate to the natural sciences can be extended by analogy to the social sciences. But in the German tradition there has been a much greater tendency to think of the social disciplines as forms of *Geisteswissenschaften* sharing essential characteristics with the humanistic disciplines" (Bernstein, 1985, p. 35).

3. The variant of hermeneutics discussed herein is the *Philosophic Hermeneutics* of Hans Georg Gadamer (1975b).

4. See chapter 2, note 13.

5. The Young Hegelians—Bauer, Bruno, Feuerbach, Hess, Marx, and Stirner (McLellan, 1969)—were among the first to reject Hegel's idealist ontology and abstract concepts in favor of a materialist ontology with correspondingly concrete categories. Marx, however, broke with the "ideologies" of the Young Hegelians, in particular with the materialism of Feuerbach, because of their attempts to isolate suprahistorical material essences, in particular a human essence that precluded the need for historical and contextual analyses. Marx's (Marx and Engels, 1947) insistence that concepts are not timeless, placeless categories but the products of a particular time and place and a particular set of *social* relations—"The human essence is no abstraction inherent in each individual. In its reality it is the ensemble of social relations" (Theses on Feuerbach, 6th thesis)—and his rejection of *essentialist, universalizing* modes of analysis are theoretical traits that postmodernists have adopted *en masse*. This raises the interesting question of whether Marx is properly considered a modernist or postmodernist, a question that certainly deserves further attention but a question the scope of which precludes the possibility of pursual within the parameters of this text.

6. This is the aspect of positivism that Popper—often referred to as a proponent of positivism—rejected out of hand, arguing that while science must be distinguished

from nonscience, that which is not scientific is not without meaning. Frisby (1972, p. 106), however, notes that Popper "did share their [the logical positivists'] interest in the foundation of an empiricist philosophy."

7. Sayer (1991, p. 144) argues that "'iron cage' is in fact an unfortunate translation" of *ein stahlhartes Gehäuse*, suggesting that "if we are to translate metaphorically, a better choice of analogy . . . might be the shell (also *Gehäuse*) on a snail's back: a burden perhaps, but something impossible to live without, in either sense of the word. A cage remains an external restraint: unlock the door, and one walks free. This *Gehäuse* is a prison altogether stronger, the armour of modern subjectivity itself."

8. See note 2.

9. See, for instance, Briton and Plumb (1992a, 1992b), Collard and Law (1989), Collins (1991), Cunningham (1989), Hart (1990), and Welton (1990, 1991, 1995).

10. While Foster is not the only commentator to divide postmodernism into two schools—cf. Rosenau (1992); Agger (1990); Gitlin (1989); Griffin (1988); Graff (1979)—his categories of "resistance" and "reaction" capture important differences between two strains of postmodernism that the categorizations of other commentators tend to muddy. Rosenau, for instance, refers to "skeptical" and "affirmative" postmodernism, assigning Continental postmodernisms to the former category, only to dismiss them out of hand as "the dark side of post-modernism, the post-modernism of despair" (p. 15). In fact, many of these postmodernisms are postmodernisms of hope, rather than despair, postmodernisms that struggle to establish an ethical, rather than an instrumental, base for action. While Foster views "postmodernisms of reaction" with suspicion, Rosenau, who includes them in her category of "affirmative post-modernisms," views them favorably, impressed by their efforts to "retain the tradition of narrative, conventional history, subject, representation and humanism" (p. 16). This is not only to overlook the oppressive nature of the traditions that "affirmative" postmodernisms support, but also to fail to recognize that what Continental postmodernisms reject when they speak of "the demise of the subject, the end of the author, the impossibility of truth, and the abrogation of the Order of Representation" (p. 15) is not the sentiments that underlie such institutions but the inherently oppressive, present-day, popular manifestation of them.

11. While Habermas (1985) does, in fact, distinguish between these two schools of postmodernism, he views both as inherently conservative, labeling those who advocate postmodernisms of resistance "young conservatives" and those who prescribe postmodernisms of reaction "neoconservatives." See also Habermas (1987).

12. See, for instance, McLaren and Hammer (1989), and Aronowitz and Giroux (1992).

13. See, for instance, Giroux (1983, 1988a, 1988b, 1988c, 1991, 1992); Giroux and McLaren (1986); McLaren (1989, 1991); and McLaren and Hammer (1989).

## CHAPTER 6. TOWARD A POSTMODERN PEDAGOGY OF ENGAGEMENT IN ADULT EDUCATION

1. This point and a number of others that follow are also made in Briton and Plumb (1992b).

2. Havel describes the Soviet *régime* that ruled the Eastern Bloc as *post*-totalitarian because, once established, it depended not on brute force and violence to impose its will, but on the more insidious practices of surveillance and intimidation.

3. According to Jhally (1989, pp. 72–73), "the *formal* subsumption [of culture] refers to a situation where an area of society becomes vital for the functioning of the economic system without actually taking on the structures of the economic system." In this situation, the system diverts capital into cultural reproduction to foster a social clime conducive to capitalist enterprise. With Gramsci (1989), Jhally contends that as long as capitalism resorts to the manipulation of culture to ensure its perpetuation, it risks being challenged. Alternate cultural practices can create interpretations, norms, roles, or institutions—counterhegemonies—to oppose capitalism's representation of the truth. The history of capitalist modernity has, in fact, been one in which anti-capitalist forces have occasionally mustered powerful campaigns to contest capitalist hegemony. The "real" subsumption of culture, however, a process facilitated by the appearance of new media technologies and corresponding marketing strategies, "refers to a situation where the media [and other cultural institutions] become not ideological institutions but economic ones. That is, investment in the media is not for the purpose of ideological control but for the purpose of reaping the biggest return. Culture is produced first and foremost as a commodity rather than as ideology." The "real" subsumption of culture begins, then, when capital from material production is diverted into cultural institutions *not* to buttress the system's representation of the truth—ideology production—and justify continued exploitive practices but to *generate* capital. Cultural production, at this point, no longer serves to augment material production but to supplement it.

4. Against those who equate the end of ideology with the end of modernity, Eagleton (1991, pp. xi–xii) argues that

> three key doctrines of postmodernist thought have conspired to discredit the classical concept of ideology. The first of these doctrines turns on a rejection of the notion of representation—in fact, a rejection of an *empiricist* model of representation, in which the representational baby has been thrown out with the empiricist bathwater. The second revolves on an epistemological scepticism which would hold that the very act of identifying any form of consciousness as ideological entails some untenable notion of absolute truth. Since the latter idea attracts few devotees these days, the former is thought to crumble in its wake. We cannot identify Pol Pot a Stalinist bigot since this would imply some metaphysical certitude about what not being a Stalinist bigot would involve. The third doctrine concerns a reformulation of the relations between rationality, interests and power, along roughly neo-Nietzschean lines, which

is thought to render the whole concept of ideology redundant. Taken together, these three theses have been thought by some enough to dispose of the whole question of ideology, at exactly the historical moment when Muslim demonstrators beat their foreheads till the blood runs, and American farmhands anticipate being swept imminently up into heaven, Cadillac and all.

5. A discussion of *some* of adult education's post-hegemonic possibilities appears in Briton and Plumb (1993a).

# Bibliography

Adorno, T. W. (ed.). (1976). *The positivist dispute in German sociology* (G. Adey and D. Frisby, trans., pp. ix–67). London, Heinemann.

Agger, B. (1990). *The decline of discourse: Reading, writing, and resistance in post-modern capitalism.* New York: Falmer Press.

Althusser, L. (1971). *Lenin and philosophy and other essays* (B. Brewster, trans.). London: New Left Books.

———. (1979). *For Marx* (B. Brewster, trans.). London: New Left Books.

———. (1992). Ideology and ideological state apparatuses. In A. Easthope and K. McGowan (eds.), *A critical and cultural theory reader* (pp. 50–58). Toronto: University of Toronto Press.

Anderson, B. (1991). *Imagined communities: Reflections on the origins and spread of nationalism* (revised). London: Verso.

Anyon, J. (1980). Social class and the hidden curriculum of work. *Journal of Education, 162,* 67–92.

Apple, M. (1979). *Ideology and curriculum.* London: Routledge and Kegan Paul.

———. (1986). *Teachers and texts: A political economy of class and gender relations in education.* New York: Routledge and Kegan Paul.

———. (1991). Introduction. In P. Lather, *Getting smart: Feminist research and pedagogy with/in the postmodern* (pp. vii–xi). New York: Routledge.

Aronowitz, S. (1988). *Science as power: Discourse and ideology in modern society.* Minneapolis: University of Minnesota Press.

———, and Giroux, H. A. (1992). *Postmodern education: Politics, culture, and social criticism.* Minneapolis: University of Minnesota Press.

Ashby, R. W. (1967). Verifiability principle. In Paul Edwards (ed.), *The encyclopedia of philosophy* (vol. 8, pp. 240–247). London: Macmillan.

Barrett, W. (1979). *The illusion of technique: A search for meaning in a technological civilization.* New York: Anchor/Doubleday.

133

Barthes, R. (1973). *Mythologies* (A. Lavers, trans.). London: Jonathon Cape.

Barton, L., Meighan, R., and Walker, S. (1980). *Schooling, ideology and curriculum.* Sussex, England: Falmer.

Baudelaire, C. (1964). The painter of modern life. In J. Mayne (trans.). *The painter of modern life and other essays.* London: Phaidon.

Baudrillard, H. (1983). *In the shadow of the silent majorities . . . or the end of the social and other essays.* New York: Semiotext(e).

Bauman, Z. (1992a). *Intimations of postmodernity.* London: Routledge.

―――. (1992b). Survival as a social construct. *Theory, culture and society, 9,* 1–36.

Baynes, K., Bohman, J., and McCarthy, T. (eds.). (1987). *After philosophy: End or transformation?* Cambridge: Massachusetts Institute of Technology Press.

Bell, D. (1973). *The coming of post-industrial society: A venture in social forecasting.* New York: Basic Books.

―――. (1976). *The cultural contradictions of capitalism.* New York: Basic Books.

Benjamin, W. (1973) *Illuminations.* (H. Zohn, trans.) New York: Harcourt, Brace & World.

Berman, M. (1982). *All that is solid melts into air: The experience of modernity.* New York: Simon and Shuster.

Bernstein, R. J. (1971). *Praxis and action: Contemporary philosophies of human activity.* Philadelphia: University of Philadelphia Press.

―――. (1985). *Beyond objectivism and relativism: Science, hermeneutics, and praxis.* Philadelphia: University of Pennsylvania Press.

Bloom, A. (1987). *The closing of the American mind.* New York: Simon and Schuster.

Bottomore, T. (1987). Hegemony. In T. Bottomore (ed.), *A dictionary of Marxist thought* (pp. 201–203). Cambridge Mass.: Harvard University Press.

Bourdieu, P., and Passeron, J. C. (1977). *Reproduction in education, society and culture.* Beverly Hills, California: Sage.

Bowles, S. and Gintis, H. (1977). *Schooling in capitalist America.* New York: Basic Books.

Bright, B. (ed.). (1989). *The epistemological imperative.* London: Croom-Helm.

Brinton, C. (1967). Enlightenment. In Paul Edwards (ed.), *The encyclopedia of philosophy* (vols. 1 and 2, pp. 519–525). London: Macmillan.

Briton, D., and Plumb, D. (1992a). Roboed: Re-imaging adult education. In the *Proceedings of the 11th Annual Conference of the Canadian Association for the Study of Adult Education* (38–43). Saskatoon, University of Saskatchewan.

————. (1992b). Václav Havel, postmodernism, and modernity: The implications for adult education in the West. In the *Proceedings of the 33rd Annual Conference of the Adult Education Research Conference* (19–24). Saskatoon, University of Saskatchewan.

————. (1993a). Remapping adult education: Post-hegemonic possibilities. In the *Proceedings of the 12th Annual Conference of the Canadian Association for the Study of Adult Education* (pp. 54–59). Faculty of Education, University of Ottawa.

————. (1993b). The commodification of adult education. In the *Proceedings of the 34th. Annual Conference of the Adult Education Research Conference* (pp. 31–36). University Park, Pennsylvania: Penn State University.

Brookfield, S. (1985). *Understanding and facilitating adult learning.* San Francisco: Jossey-Bass.

————. (1989). The epistemology of adult education in the United States and Great Britain: A cross-cultural analysis. In B. Bright (ed.), *The epistemological imperative* (pp. 141–173). London: Croom-Helm.

————. (1990). Analyzing the influence of media on learners' perspectives. In J. Mezirow and Associates (eds.), *Fostering critical reflection in adulthood: A guide to emancipatory learning* (pp. 235–250). San Francisco: Jossey-Bass.

———— (ed.). (1987). *Learning democracy: Eduard Lindeman on adult education and social change.* London: Croom Helm.

Burkitt, I. (1991). Social selves: Theories of the social formation of personality. *Monographs of the Journal of the International Sociological Association, 39*(6). London: Sage.

Butler, J. (1987). *Gender trouble.* New York: Routledge.

Campfens, H. (1991). *Nurturing community: The individual and community in development practice.* Keynote address to the Community Development Conference of the Edmonton Social Planning Council, Alberta, Canada.

Castoriadis, C. (1987). *The imaginary institution of society* (K. Blamey, trans.). Cambridge: Polity Press.

Carr, W., and Kemmis, S. (1986). *Becoming critical: Education, knowledge and action research.* London: Falmer.

Cervero, R. M., and Wilson, A. L. (1994). *Planning responsibly for adult education: A guide to negotiating power and interests.* San Francisco: Jossey Bass.

Clifford, J. (1989). Notes on travel and theory. In J. Clifford and V. Dhareshwar (eds.), *Travelling theories, travelling theorists.* Santa Cruz: University of California Press.

Collard, S., and Law, M. (1989). The limits of perspective transformation: A critique of Mezirow's theory. *Adult Education Quarterly, 39*(2), 99–107.

Collins, M. (1987). Self-directed learning and the misappropriation of adult education practice. In the *Proceedings of the 6th Annual Conference of the Canadian Association for the Study of Adult Education*. Hamilton, Canada: McMaster University Press.

————. (1988). Prison education: A substantial metaphor for adult education practice. *Adult Education Quarterly, 38*(2), 101–110.

————. (1991). *Adult education as vocation: A critical role for the adult educator.* London: Routledge.

————. (1992). *Current trends in adult education: From self-directed learning to critical theory.* Paper presented to the 6th Annual Meeting of the Association of Process Philosophy of Education, American Philosophical Association, Annual Meetings, Kentucky.

Copleston, F. C. (1985). *A history of philosophy* (book 2, vol. 4). New York: Image Books.

Corrigan, P. R. (1991). The making of the boy: Meditations on what grammar school did with, to, and for my body. In H. A. Giroux (ed.), *Postmodernism, feminism and cultural politics* (pp. 196–216). Albany: State University of New York Press.

Crary, J. (1990). *Techniques of the observer: On vision & modernity in the nineteenth century.* Cambridge: Massachusettes Institute of Technology Press.

Cruikshank, J. (1991). Ethical issues in university extension work. In the *Proceedings of the 10th annual conference of the Canadian Association for the Study of Adult Education* (pp. 57–62). Kingston, Ontario: Queen's University.

Cunningham, P. M. (1989). Making a more significant impact on society. In A. Quigley (ed.), *New directions for continuing education: Fulfilling the promise of adult and continuing education* (pp. 33–46). San Francisco: Jossey-Bass.

————. (1992). University continuing educators should be social activists. *Canadian Journal of University and Continuing Education, 28*(2), 9–17.

Darkenwald, G. G., and Merriam, S. B. (1982). *Adult education: Foundations of practice.* New York: Harper and Row.

de Saussure, F. (1974). *Course in general linguistics* (W. Baskin, trans.). London: Fontana.

Dear, M. J., and Wolch, J. R. (1991). How territory shapes social life. In M. J. Dear and J. R. Wolch (eds.), *The power of geography: How territory shapes social life* (pp. 3–18). Boston: Unwin Hyman.

Debord, G. (1990). *Comments on the society of the spectacle.* (M. Imrie, trans.). London: Verso.

Eagleton, R. (1991). *Ideology: An introduction.* London: Verso.

Easthope, A., and McGowan, K. (eds.). (1992). *A critical and cultural theory reader.* Toronto: University of Toronto Press.

Eisner, E., W. (1983). Anastasia might still be alive, but the monarchy is dead. *Educational Researcher, 12*(5), 13–24.

Elias, N. (1978). *The civilizing process*: vol. 1, *The history of manners* (E. Jephcott, trans.). New York: Urizen Books.

Ellsworth, E. (1989). Why doesn't this feel empowering? Working through the repressive myths of critical pedagogy. *Harvard Educational Review, 59*(3), 297–324.

Fay, B. (1975). *Social theory and political practice.* London: Allen and Unwin.

Feyerabend, P. (1988). *Against method: Outline of an anarchist theory of knowledge* (2d ed.). New York: Verso.

Fieldhouse, R. (1981). The ideological parameters of adult education in England, 1925–1950. In the *Proceedings of the 22nd. Adult Education Research Conference* (pp. 79–85). DeKalb: Northern Illinois University.

Finger, M. (1988). Hermeneutics, critical theory and biographical method as an alternative in adult education. In *The Proceedings of trans Atlantic Dialogue: A Research Exchange.* (pp. 166–171). Leeds: School of Continuing Education, University of Leeds.

Fiske, J. (1992). *Introduction to communication studies* (2d ed.). New York: Routledge.

Foster, H (1985). Postmodernism: A preface to *The anti-aesthetic: Essays on postmodern culture.* Port Townsend, Washington: Bay Press.

Foster, H. (1989). Wild signs (The breakup of the sign in seventies' art). In J. Tagg (ed.), *The cultural politics of "postmodernism": Current debates in art history: One* (pp. 13–31). Binghamton: State University of New York.

Foster, H. (1992). Readings in cultural resistance. In H. Foster, *Recodings: Art, spectacle, cultural politics* (pp. 157–179). Seattle, Washington: Bay Press.

Foucault, M. (1970). *The order of things.* London: Tavistock.

———. (1972). *The archaeology of knowledge* (A. M. Sheridan Smith, trans.). London: Tavistock.

———. (1977). *Discipline and punish* (A. Sheridan, trans.). London: Allen Lane.

———. (1982). The subject and power. *Critical inquiry, 8,* 777–795.

———. (1984). What is enlightenment? In P. Rabinow (ed.), *The Foucault reader* (pp. 32–50). New York: Pantheon.

———. (1988), History of systems of thought. In D. F. Bouchard (ed.), *Language, counter-memory, practice: Selected essays and interviews with Michel Foucault* (pp. 199–204). Ithaca, New York: Cornell University Press.

Freire, P. (1974). *Pedagogy of the oppressed* (M. B. Ramos, trans.). New York: Continuum.

Frisby, D. (1972). The Popper-Adorno controversy: The methodological dispute in German Sociology. *Philosophy of Social Science, 2,* 105–119.

———. (1976). Introduction. In T. W. Adorno (ed.), *The Positivist dispute in German sociology.* (G. Adey and D. Frisby, trans., pp. ix–67). London: Heinemann.

Gadamer, H. G. (1975a). Hermeneutics and social science. *Cultural Hermeneutics, 2,* 307–316.

———. (1975b). *Truth and method.* (G. Barden and J Cunningham, trans.). New York: Seabury.

———. (1976). *Philosophical hermeneutics.* (D. E. Linge, trans.). Berkeley: University of California Press.

———. (1979). The problem of historical consciousness. In P. Rabinow and W. M. Sullivan (eds.), *Interpretive social science: A reader.* Berkeley: University of California Press.

Geertz, C. (1979). From the native's point of view: On the nature of anthropological understanding. In P. Rabinow and W. M. Sullivan (eds.), *Interpretive social science: A reader.* Berkeley: University of California Press.

Geras, N. (1987). Althusser, L. In T. Bottomore (ed.), *A dictionary of Marxist thought* (pp. 15–18). Cambridge, Mass.: Harvard University Press.

Giroux, H. A. (1981). *Ideology, culture and the process of schooling.* Philadelphia: Temple University Press.

———. (1983). *Theory and resistance in education.* Granby, Mass.: Bergin and Garvey.

———. (1988a). Postmodernism and the discourse of educational criticism. *Journal of Education, 170*(3), 5–30.

———. (1988b). *Schooling and the struggle for public life: Critical pedagogy in the modern age.* Minneapolis: University of Minnesota Press.

———. (1988c). *Teachers as intellectuals: Toward a critical pedagogy of learning.* Granby, Mass.: Bergin and Garvey.

———. (1992). *Border crossings: Cultural workers and the politics of education.* New York: Routledge.

——— (ed.). (1991). *Postmodernism, feminism, and cultural politics.* Albany: State University of New York Press.

———, and McLaren, P. (1986). Teacher education and the politics of engagement: The case for democratic schooling. *Harvard Educational Review, 56*(3), 213–38.

Gitlin, T. (1989). Postmodernism: Roots and politics. *Dissent* (Winter), 100–108.

Gore, J. M. (1993). *The struggle for pedagogies: Critical and feminist discourses as regimes of truth*. London: Routledge.

Gouldner, A. W. (1970). *The coming crisis in Western sociology*. New York: Basic Books.

Graff, G. (1979). *Literature against itself*. Chicago: University of Chicago Press.

Gramsci, Antonio (1989). *Selections from the prison notebooks of Antonio Gramsci* (Quintin Hoare and Geoffrey Newell Smith, eds. and trans.). New York: International Publishers.

Grave, S. A. (1967). Common sense. In P. Edwards (ed.), *The Encyclopedia of philosophy* (vol. 2, pp. 155–160). New York: Macmillan.

Greene, M. (1990). Realizing literature's emancipatory potential. In J. Mezirow and Associates (eds.), *Fostering critical reflection in adulthood: A guide to emancipatory learning* (pp. 252–268). San Francisco: Jossey-Bass.

Griffin, D. R. (1988). *The reenchantment of science: Postmodern proposals*. Albany: State University of New York Press.

Habermas, J. (1972). *Knowledge and human interests* (J. J. Shapiro, trans.). London: Heinemann.

———. (1975). *Legitimation crisis*. (T. McCarthy, trans.). Boston: Beacon.

———. (1984). *The theory of communicative action* (vols. 1 and 2, T. McCarthy, trans.). Boston: Beacon.

———. (1985). Modernity—An incomplete project. In H. Foster (ed.), *The anti-aesthetic: Essays on postmodern culture*. Port Townsend, Washington: Bay Press.

———. (1987). *The philosophical discourse of modernity*. (F. Lawrence, trans.). Cambridge: Massachusetts Institute of Technology Press.

Halévy, E. (1986). *Thomas Hodgskin*. London: Ernest Benn.

Hall, S. (1991). Ethnicity: Identity and difference. *Radical America*, *23*(4), 9–20.

———. (1992). Cultural studies and its theoretical legacies. In L. Grossberg, N. Nelson, and P. Treichler (eds.), *Cultural studies* (pp. 277–294). New York: Routledge.

Hart, M. (1985). Thematization of power, the search for common interests, and self-reflection: Towards a comprehensive concept of emancipatory education. *International Journal of Lifelong Learning*, *4*(2), 119–134.

———. (1990a). Critical theory and beyond: Perspectives on emancipatory education. *Adult Education Quarterly*, *40*(3).

————. (1990b). Liberation through consciousness raising. In J. Mezirow and Associates (eds.), *Fostering critical reflection in adulthood: A guide to emancipatory learning* (pp. 47–73). San Francisco: Jossey-Bass.

Harvey, D. (1989). *The condition of postmodernity: An enquiry into the origins of cultural change*. Oxford: Basil Blackwell.

Havel, V. (1978). The power of the powerless. In J. Vladislav (ed.), *Living in the truth* (pp. 36–122). London: Faber and Faber.

————. (1990). Growing up "outside." In P. Wilson (trans.), *Disturbing the peace* (pp. 3–33). New York: Vintage Books.

Heaney, T. W., and Horton, A. I. (1990). Reflective engagement for social change. In J. Mezirow and Associates (eds.), *Fostering critical reflection in adulthood: A guide to emancipatory learning* (pp. 74–98). San Francisco: Jossey-Bass.

Hearn, F. (1985). *Reason and freedom in sociological thought*. Boston: Allen and Unwin.

Hebdige, D. (1979). *Subculture: The meaning of style*. New York: Routledge.

Hegel, G. W. F. (1974). *Hegel: The essential writings* (F. G. Weiss, ed.). New York: Harper.

Heidegger, M. (1959). *Introduction to metaphysics* (R. Mannheim, trans.). New Haven: Yale University Press.

————. (1962). *Being and time* (J. Macquarrie and E. Robinson, trans.). London: SCM Press.

————. (1977). *The question concerning technology, and other essays* (W. Lovitt, trans.). New York: Garland.

Hellyer, M., and Schied, F. (1984). Workers' education and the labor college movement: Radical traditions in American adult education. In the *Proceedings of the 24th Annual Adult Education Research Conference* (pp. 82–87). Raliegh: North Carolina State University.

Hesse, M. (1980). *Revolution and reconstruction in the philosophy of science*. Bloomington: Indiana University Press.

Hoogvelt, A. M. M. (1982). *The third world in global development*. London: Macmillan.

Horkheimer, M., and Adorno, T. W. (1978). *Dialectic of enlightenment*. New York: Herder and Herder.

Howard, D. (1977). *The Marxian legacy*. New York: Urizen Books.

————. (1988). *The politics of critique*. Minneapolis: University of Minnesota Press.

Jameson, F. (1984). Postmodernism, or the cultural logic of late capitalism. *New Left Review, July–August*(146), 53–92.

———. (1989). Foreward. In . F. Lyotard, *The postmodern condition: A report on knowledge*. (G. Bennington and B. Massumi, trans.). Minneapolis: University of Minnesota Press.

———. (1992) *Postmodernism, or the cultural logic of late capitalism*. Durham: Duke University Press.

Jhally, S. (1989). The political economy of culture. In I. Angus and S. Jhally (eds.), *Cultural politics in contemporary America*. New York: Routledge.

Kant, I. (1983). An answer to the question: What is enlightenment? In T. Humphrey (trans.), *Perpetual peace and other essays* (pp. 41–48). Indianapolis, Indiana: Hackett.

Keat, R. (1981). *The politics of social theory: Habermas, Freud and the critique of positivism*. Chicago: Basil Blackwell.

Kellner, D. (1990). Critical theory and the crisis of social theory. *Sociological Perspectives, 33*(1), 11–33.

———. (1992). Constructing postmodern identities. In S. Lash and J. Friedman (eds.), *Modernity and identity* (pp. 141–177). Cambridge, Mass.: Blackwell.

Kidd, J. R. (ed.). (1961). Preface. In E. C. Lindeman, *The meaning of adult education* (pp. xiii–xxiv). Montreal: Harvest House.

Kim, Y. S. (1991). *The nihilistic challenge to curriculum and pedagogy*. Unpublished doctoral dissertation, University of Alberta.

Kipnis, L. (1992). (Male) desire and (female) disgust: Reading Hustler. In L. Grossberg, C. Nelson, and P. A. Treichler (eds.), *Cultural studies* (pp. 373–391). New York: Routledge.

Kuhn, T. S. (1970). *The structure of scientific revolutions* (2d. ed.). Chicago: The University of Chicago Press.

Lacan, J. (1977a). *The four fundamental concepts of psycho-analysis* (J-A. Miller, ed., and A. Sheridan, trans.). London: Hogarth.

———. (1977b). The mirror stage as formative of the function of the I as revealed in psychoanalytic experience. In J. Lacan, *Écrits: A selection* (A. Sheridan, trans.). London, Tavistock.

Laclau, E., and Mouffe, C. (1985). *Hegemony and socialist* strategy: *Towards a radical democratic politics*. London: Verso.

———. (1990). Post-Marxism without apologies. In E. Laclau, *New reflections on the revolution of our time* (pp. 97–132). London: Verso.

Lakatos, I. (1970). Falsification and the methodology of scientifc research programmes. In I. Lakatos and A. Musgrave (eds.), *Criticism and the growth of knowledge*. Cambridge: Cambridge University Press.

Langford, L. L. (1992). Postmodernism and enlightenment, or, why not a fascist aesthetics? *Substance, 67*, 24–43.

Larrain, J. (1987). Idealism and ideology. In T. Bottomore (ed.), *A dictionary of Marxist thought* (pp. 218–223). Cambridge, Mass.: Harvard University Press.

——. (1989). *Theories of development: Capitalism, colonialism and dependency.* Cambridge, England: Polity.

Lasch, C. (1979). *The culture of narcissism: American life in an age of diminishing expectations.* New York: Warner Books.

Lash, S. (1990). *Sociology of postmodernism.* New York: Routledge.

——, and Urry, J. (1987). *The end of organized capitalism.* Cambridge: Polity Press.

Lather, P. (1986). Issues of validity in openly ideological research: Between a rock and a soft place. *Harvard Educational Review, 17*(4), 63–84.

——. (1991). *Getting smart: Feminist research and pedagogy with/in the postmodern.* New York: Routledge.

Law, M. (1992). Engels, Marx, and radical adult education: A rereading of a tradition. In the *Proceedings of the 33rd Annual Conference of the Adult Education Research Conference* (150–158). Saskatoon, University of Saskatchewan.

——, and Rubenson, K. (1988). Andragogy: The return of the Jedi. In M. Zukas (ed.), *Proceedings of trans Atlantic Dialogue: A Research Exchange.* (pp. 232–237). Leeds: School of Continuing Education, University of Leeds.

Lefebvre, H. (1991). *The production of space* (D. Nicholson-Smith, trans.). Oxford: Blackwell.

Levi-Strauss, C. (1975). *The raw and the cooked.* New York: Harper and Row.

Lindeman, E. C. (1929a). Characteristics of adult education. In S. Brookfield (ed.), *Learning democracy: Eduard Lindeman on adult education and social change* (pp. 37–38). London: Croom Helm.

——. (1929b). The meaning of adult learning. In S. Brookfield (ed.), *Learning democracy: Eduard Lindeman on adult education and social change* (pp. 29–36). London: Croom Helm.

——. (1932). International aspects of adult education. In S. Brookfield (ed.), *Learning democracy: Eduard Lindeman on adult education and social change* (pp. 69–74). London: Croom Helm.

——. (1935a). Reaffirming the democratic process. In S. Brookfield (ed.), *Learning democracy: Eduard Lindeman on adult education and social change* (pp. 137–145). London: Croom Helm.

——. (1935b). The place of discussion in the learning process. In S. Brookfield (ed.), *Learning democracy: Eduard Lindeman on adult education and social change* (pp. 43–47). London: Croom Helm.

———. (1937). Adult education for social change. In S. Brookfield (ed.), *Learning democracy: Eduard Lindeman on adult education and social change* (pp. 75–77). London: Croom Helm.

———. (1938a). Group work and democracy. In S. Brookfield (ed.), *Learning democracy: Eduard Lindeman on adult education and social change* (pp. 146–151). London: Croom Helm.

———. (1938b). Preparing leaders in adult education. In S. Brookfield (ed.), *Learning democracy: Eduard Lindeman on adult education and social change* (pp. 48–52). London: Croom Helm.

———. (1944a). Adult education and the democratic discipline. In S. Brookfield (ed.), *Learning democracy: Eduard Lindeman on adult education and social change* (pp. 158–162). London: Croom Helm.

———. (1944b). Democracy and the friendship pattern. In S. Brookfield (ed.), *Learning democracy: Eduard Lindeman on adult education and social change* (pp. 152–157). London: Croom Helm.

———. (1944c). New needs for adult education. In S. Brookfield (ed.), *Learning democracy: Eduard Lindeman on adult education and social change* (pp. 101–112). London: Croom Helm.

———. (1944d). Education for racial understanding. In S. Brookfield (ed.), *Learning democracy: Eduard Lindeman on adult education and social change* (pp. 93–100). London: Croom Helm.

———. (1945a). The sociology of adult education. In S. Brookfield (ed.), *Learning democracy: Eduard Lindeman on adult education and social change* (pp. 113–121). London: Croom Helm.

———. (1945b). World peace through adult education. In S. Brookfield (ed.), *Learning democracy: Eduard Lindeman on adult education and social change* (pp. 122–124). London: Croom Helm.

———. (1947). Methods of democratic adult education. In S. Brookfield (ed.), *Learning democracy: Eduard Lindeman on adult education and social change* (pp. 53–59). London: Croom Helm.

———. (1949). Democracy and *The Meaning of Adult Education*. In S. Brookfield (ed.), *Learning democracy: Eduard Lindeman on adult education and social change* (pp. 177–179). London: Croom Helm.

———. (1961). *The meaning of adult education*. Montreal: Harvest House.

Lovitt, W. (1977). Introduction. In M. Heidegger, The *question concerning technology, and other essays* (pp. xiii–xxxix). New York: Garland.

Löwith, K. (1982). *Max Weber and Karl Marx* (T. Bottomore and W. Outhwaite, eds., H. Fantel, trans.). London: George Allen and Unwin.

Lyotard, J. F. (1988). *The differend: Phrases in dispute.* Minneapolis: University of Minnesota Press.

————. (1989). *The postmodern condition: A report on knowledge.* (G. Bennington and B. Massumi, trans.). Minneapolis: University of Minnesota Press.

Marcuse, H. (1964). *One dimensional man: Studies in the ideology of advanced industrial society.* Boston: Beacon.

Marx, K. (1983a). The communist manifesto. In E. Kamenka (ed.), *The portable Karl Marx* (pp. 203–217). Kingsport, Tennessee: Penguin.

————. (1983b). The eighteenth brumaire of Louis Bonaparte. In E. Kamenka (ed.), *The portable Karl Marx* (pp. 287–323). Kingsport, Tennessee: Penguin.

————. (1989). *Readings from Karl Marx.* (D. Sayer, ed.). New York: Routledge.

————, and Engels, F. (1947). *The German ideology* (rev. ed.). New York: International Publishers.

McLaren, P. (1989). *Life in schools: An introduction to critical pedagogy.* New York: Longman.

————. (1991). Schooling the postmodern body: Critical pedagogy and the politics of enfleshment. In H. A. Giroux (ed.), *Postmodernism, feminism, and cultural politics* (pp. 144–173). Albany: State University of New York Press.

————. (1993). Multiculturalism and the postmodern critique: Towards a pedagogy of resistance and transformation. *Cultural Studies, 7*(1), 118–146.

————, and Hammer, R. (1989). Critical pedagogy and the postmodern challenge: Towards a critical postmodernist pedagogy of liberation. *Educational Foundations, 3*(3), 29–62.

McLellan, D. (1969). *The young Hegellians and Karl Marx.* London: Macmillan.

Mead, G. H. (1981). *Selected writings.* (J. R. Andrews, ed.). Chicago: University of Chicago Press.

Mennell, S. (1992). *Norbert Elias: An introduction.* London: Blackwell.

Metz, C. (1982). *The imaginary signifier: Psychoanalysis and the cinema* (C. Britton, A. Williams, B. Brewster, & A. Guzzetti, trans.). Bloomington: Indiana University Press.

Mezirow, J. (1985). Concept and action in adult education. *Adult Education Quarterly, 35*, 142–151.

————. (1990). How critical reflection triggers transformative learning. In J. Mezirow and Associates (eds.), *Fostering critical reflection in adulthood: A guide to emancipatory learning* (pp. 1–20). San Francisco: Jossey-Bass.

Mills, C. W. (1959). *The sociological imagination*. New York: Oxford University Press.

Namenwirth, M. (1986). Science through a feminist prism. In R. Bleir (ed.), *Feminist approaches to science* (pp. 18–41). New York: Permagon.

Nidditch, P. H. (1975). Foreword. In P. H. Nidditch (ed.), *John Locke: an essay concerning human understanding* (pp. vii–xxvi). Oxford: Clarendon.

Nietzsche, F. (1968). *The will to power*. (W. Kaufmann, ed., W. Kaufmann and R. J. Hollingdale, trans.). New York: Vintage.

———. (1974). *The gay science*. (W. Kaufmann, trans.). New York: Vintage Books.

Ohliger, J. (1990). Alternative images of the future in adult education. In S. B. Merriam and P. M. Cunningham (eds.), *Handbook of adult and continuing education* (pp. 628–639). San Francisco: Jossey-Bass.

Ollman, B. (1990). *Alienation: Marx's concept of man in capitalist society* (2d ed.). New York: Cambridge University Press.

Parsons, T., and Platt, G. M. (1973). *The American university*. Cambridge, Mass.: Harvard University Press.

Patton, M. Q. (1975). *Alternative evaluation research paradigms*. Grand Forks: University of North Dakota Press.

Phelan, S. (1989). *Identity politics: Lesbian feminism and the limits of community*. Philadelphia: Temple University Press.

Plumb, D. T. (1989). *The significance of Jürgen Habermas for the pedagogy of Paulo Freire and the practice of adult education*. Unpublished master's thesis, University of Saskatchewan.

Popkewitz, T. S. (1992). Culture, pedagogy, and power: Issues in the production of values and colonization. In K. Weiler and Y. C. Mitchell (eds.), *What schools can do: Critical pedagogy and practice*. (pp. 133–148). Albany: State University of New York Press.

Popper, K. R. (1988). *The open society and its enemies: The high tide of prophecy; Hegel, Marx and the aftermath* (4th ed.). London: Routledge and Kegan Paul.

Poster, M. (1990). *The mode of information: Poststructuralism and social context*. Cambridge: Polity Press.

Richters, A. (1988). Modernity-postmodernity controversies: Habermas and Foucault. *Theory, Culture and Society*, 5, 611–643.

Rockhill, K. (1984). Between the wars: Liberalism and the eclipsing of conflict in the framing of adult education. In the *Proceedings of the 24th Annual Adult Education Research Conference* (pp. 159–164). Raliegh: North Carolina State University.

———, Carlson, R., and Davenport, S. (1982). The revisionist perspective: A critical look at the history of adult education in the United States. In the *Proceedings of the 23rd Annual Adult Education Research Conference* (pp. 248–253). Lincoln: University of Nebraska.

Roman, L. G. (1993). "On the ground" with antiracist pedagogy and Raymond Williams's unfinished project to articulate a socially transformative critical realism. In D. L. Dworkin and L. G. Roman (eds.), *Views beyond the border country: Raymond Williams and cultural politics.* New York: Routledge.

Rosenau, P. M. (1992). *Post-modernism and the social sciences: Insights, inroads, and intrusions.* Princeton, New Jersey: Princeton University Press.

Rubenson, K. (1990). The sociology of adult education. In S. Merriam and P. Cunningham (eds.), Handbook of adult and continuing education (pp. 51–69). San Francisco: Jossey-Bass.

Sayer, D. (1991). *Capitalism and modernity: An excursus on Marx and Weber.* London: Routledge.

Schied, F. M. (1992). Connecting workers' education to the working class: Labor schools and informal learning in cultural context. In the Proceedings *of the 33rd Annual Conference of the Adult Education Research Conference* (221–227). Saskatoon, University of Saskatchewan.

———. (1993). *Learning in social context: Workers and adult education in nineteenth-century Chicago.* DeKalb, Illinois: LEPS Press, Northern Illinois University.

Seidman, S. (1989). Introduction. In S. Seidman (ed.), *Jürgen Habermas on society and politics: A reader.* Boston: Beacon.

Stewart, D. W. (1984). A review of *The Meaning of Adult Education.* In M. Collins (ed.), *The 1984 Adult learning review of books* (pp. 1–12). Manhattan, Kansas: Learning Resources Network.

Tagg, J. (1992). *Grounds of dispute: Art history, cultural politics and the discursive field.* Minneapolis: University of Minnesota Press.

Taylor, C. (1987). Overcoming epistemology. In K. Baynes, J. Bohman, and T. McCarthy (eds.), *After philosophy: End or transformation?* (pp. 464–488). Cambridge: Massachusetts Institute of Technology Press.

———. (1992). *The malaise of modernity.* Ontario: Anansi.

Taylor, R., Rockhill, K., and Fieldhouse, R. (1985). *University adult education in England and the United States: A reappraisal of the liberal tradition.* London: Croom Helm.

Thompson, J. L. (1980). Adult education and the disadvantaged. In J. L. Thompson (ed.), *Adult education for a change* (pp. 83–108). London: Hutchinson.

Thorpe, M., Edwards, R., and Hanson, A. (eds.). (1993). *Culture and processes of adult learning: A reader.* London: Routledge.

Tomlinson, J. (1991). *Cultural imperialism: A critical introduction*. Baltimore, Md.: Johns Hopkins University Press.

Usher, R. (1989). *Adult education as theory, practice, and research: The captive triangle*. London: Routledge.

Usher, R., and Edwards, R. (1994). *Postmodernism and education*. London: Routledge.

Vattimo, G. (1990). Postmodern criticism: Postmodern critique. In D. Woods (ed.), *Writing the future*. London: Verso.

Warren, M. E. (1988). *Nietzsche and political thought*. Cambridge: Massachusetts Institute of Technology Press.

Weber, M. (1978). *Economy and society* (vol. 1, G. Roth and C. Wittich, eds.). Berkeley: University of California Press.

———. (1979). *From Max Weber: Essays in sociology*. (H. Garth and C. W. Mills, eds. and trans.). New York: Oxford University Press.

Welton, M. R. (1991). Dangerous knowledge: Canadian workers' education in the decades of discord. *Studies in the Education of Adults*, *23*(1), 25–40.

——— (ed.). (1987a). *Knowledge for the people: The struggle for adult learning on English-speaking Canada, 1828–1973*. Toronto: Ontario Institute for the Study of Education Press.

———. (1987b). On the eve of a great mass movement: Reflections on the origins of the CAAE. In F. Cassidy and R. Ferris (eds.), *Choosing our future: Adult education and public policy in Canada*. Toronto: Ontario Institute for the Study of Education Press.

——— (ed.). (1995). *In defense of the lifeworld: Critical perspectives on adult learning*. New York: State University of New York Press.

Westwood, S., and Thomas, J. E. (eds.). (1991). *Radical agendas?: The politics of adult education*. Leicester: National Institute of Adult and Continuing Education.

Wexler, P. (1987). *Social analysis of education: After the new sociology*. New York: Routledge and Kegan Paul.

Whitty, G., and Young, M. (1977). *Society, state and schooling*. Sussex, England: Palmer.

Williams, R. (1961). *The long revolution*. New York: Columbia University Press.

Williams, Raymond (1958). *Culture and society*. London: Hogarth Press.

Willis, P. (1983). Cultural production and theories of reproduction. In L. Barton and S. Walker (eds.), *Race, class and education*. London: Croom-Helm.

Wilson, A. L. (1991). *Epistemological foundations of American adult education, 1934 to 1989: A study of knowledge and interests*. Unpublished doctoral dissertation, University of Georgia, Athens.

————. (1992). Science and the professionalization of American adult education, 1934–1989: A study of knowledge development in the adult education handbooks. In the *Proceedings of the 33rd Annual Adult Education Research Conference* (pp. 260–267). Saskatoon: University of Saskatchewan.

Wiseman, M. B. (1989). *The ecstacies of Roland Barthes*. New York: Routledge.

Wolin, R. (1985). Modernism vs postmodernism. *Telos, 62*, 9–29.

Zacharakis-Jutz, J. (1989). "Straight to the heart of the union": Workers' education in the United Packinghouse Workers of America, 1951–1953. In the *Proceedings of the 30th Annual Adult Education Research Conference* (pp. 273–279). Madison: University of Wisconsin.

————. (1992). "Education for what?": A notion of liberal adult education in the 1950s. In the *Proceedings of the 33rd Annual Conference of the Adult Education Research Conference* (150–158). Saskatoon, University of Saskatchewan.

Žižek, S. (1992). *The sublime object of ideology*. London: Verso.

# Index

149

means of:
 production 69; subsistence 69
Mennell, S. 72
meta-narratives 81
metaphysical:
 certainties 71, 100; dogmas 57;
 essences 96; position 74; thinking 70
metaphysics:
 of Descartes 75; set aside by modernity 116; rejection of 65
method:
 dialectical 82; dialogical 80
methodological rules 46
Middle Ages 59, 72, 75
Mills, C. Wright 87
model of knowledge 34
modern:
 age 74; alienated self 67; atomism 46;
 bourgeois society 67; conception of
 science 75; consciousness 115; disengaged identity 65; individual 67;
 instrumental practice of adult education xi; notion of self 69, 70; notion of
 the subject 67, 74; science 47, 101;
 scientific paradigm 54; scientific rationality 84; scientific worldview 81; self
 73; subject 72, 76; technological age
 74; way of knowing 75
modernism 93:
 cultural 91; cultural forces of 92
modernist vision of West 103
modernity 56, 57, 58, 60, 64, 67:
 advent of 75; attitude of 57; as consequence of 111; end of 108; greatest
 achievement of 111; ideals of 97;
 impersonal forces of 111, 115; oppressive forces of 105; painful lessons of
 116; project of 62, 63, 94; rational
 vision of progress of 104; scientific
 rationality of 110; systematizing
 impulse of 104; three features of 114;
 totalizing narratives of 94; true origin
 of 74
modernization 20, 68:
 capitalist 91; ills of 93

modes of inquiry:
 alternative 80; critical x, 95; critical
 postmodern x, 94; dialogical 95;
 empirical-analytic 79, 83; interpretive
 x, 79; positivist x, 79, 83; postmodern
 x, 79, 83, 92, 93, 97
monad 77
myths 40

Namenwirth, M. 29, 30
narcissism:
 seeds of 112
narcissistic:
 ethos 107
natural rights of Man 66
natural scientific method 61
nature:
 scientific domination of 62
*Naturwissenschaften* 80, 88
negation:
 and critical postmodernism 94
neo-Marxism 95, 96
neoconservative 92:
 postmodernisms of reaction 94; reactionaries 100
neo-Classicism 72
Newton's *Principia* 60
Newtonian physics 37
Nidditch, P.H. 58
Nietzsche F. x, 29, 37, 67, 70, 71, 87, 89
nihilism:
 and postmodernism of resistance 116
normal science 45, 46, 50

Ohliger, John 14
Ollman, Bertell 82
operationalism 21, 22
operationalize 27
operationalized 37
oppressive social forms 97
oppressive structures 90

paradigm(s) 45, 47, 50